From Grief to Goodness

by

ALISHA THORPE

DR. NES INTERNATIONAL CONSULTING & PUBLISHING

PASADENA, CA LOS ANGELES, CA

Dr. Nes International Consulting & Publishing
P.O. Box 70167
Pasadena, CA 91117.
www.drnesintl.com

The book recounts certain events in the life of Alisha Thorpe according to her recollection and perspective. This purpose of this book is not to defame, but to empower and motivate readers to pursue the goodness that can came after loss.

ISBN: 9780999178560

Senior Editor: Femi Fletcher

Cover Design: Jessica Land

ACKNOWLEDGEMENTS

This book is dedicated to people all over the world - every race, every ethnicity, young and old alike – anyone who is going through grief or depression. If you feel like you can't go on, I pray that God moves you into everything He has for you, and that you become all He made you to be.

First and foremost, I would like to thank God, who is the head of my life, because I couldn't do anything without You and I love You. In the process of writing this book, I realized this was a part of my healing. Thank You for giving me the vision and the faith to birth this book. I could never have done this without the faith I have in You, the Almighty. I will keep close to my heart Psalm 23:1-6. Always.

To my wonderful husband, Elder Howard Tyrone Thorpe, I thank you for your love and prayers and your great cooking, but especially for the Word you shared with me throughout our marriage. I love you so much and I miss you. GOD, YOU, AND ME.

To my spiritual father, Pastor Monty and First Lady Kim Weatherall, I thank you for the Kingdom teaching that you give every Saturday and Sunday, and for the love you have always shown us. We are so grateful to be sitting under Love Church.

To my spiritual parents, Evangelists Ernest & Jeraldine Doss; Dr. John and Cathy Moore; and Reverend Margaret Smith, I thank you for your prayers, support, and the love you have shown me, and I am forever grateful to you all as prayer partners and friends. I love you.

To my children, Davida and Malcom, to Veronica and my son-in-law Tony: you're an inspiration to me. Thank you for all the love and support you have given me and for my grandchildren, whom I love dearly.

To my faithful prayer sisters, Minister Janice, Latrice, Tammy, Imani, Sheila, Tina, Donna, Freda, Monica, Cynthia Jenkins, Monique, Jackie, Wanda, Evangelist Shirley, Dr. Rochelle, Lillian and to my Faith family friends: I don't know where I would be without my prayer warriors. I pray God will to continue to bless each one of you.

I must give thanks to my wonderful family. My parents: Ulysses Jr & Priscilla Tobias and To my siblings Kevin & Sylvia, George & Christina, Paul, Ulysses, Clarence and my Grandparents Ulysses & Gertrude Tobias;

law Pastor Andrew & Ruth Prowell, Johnnie & Latrice Brimmage; my sisters-in-law Idella Gale and Mary Lou Thorpe; to Elder Jerald & Cynthia Jenkins, Aaren & Carmen Smith, Mike & Juliana Tsasa, Derricus & Leah Wood, and Otis & Donna Lumpkin, Jon & Janis Flakes, Jeffrey & Carmen Hoffmann, & Minister Janice Weems: Thank you all for all the love you showed my husband and me during his illness and for your continued prayers and the encouraging words and support. As you all know, family is everything to me and I will love you all always and forever.

To Pastor Ronnie and First Lady Wanda Williams, Pastors Andre and Albertina Downing, Pastor Roderick and First Lady Melanie Walker, Pastor Dejuan and First Lady Kim Weatherall, Pastor Mark & Juanita Gullet, Pastor Willis and First Lady Lashawn Thompson , Elder Charles and Rebecca McClain, Elders Ronald & Petra Cooper, Sredrick and Imani Robinson, Gerald and Sheila Thomas, Chief Apostles Darrell and Vera Roberts, and Apostles Eddie and Lizzie Stallings: I would like to thank you for all the support that you showed to Elder Tyrone and me, and we love you. Always keep giving those words of encouragement.

To the Ministry Teen: Keep dancing for the Lord and know that God is pleased with you. You don't know how many people you have blessed; I am one of them. I love you Iyanna, Devin, and Jada.

To all our church Family at Love Church, to all our family and friends who were there for us during Elder Tyrone's illness, passing, and during my bereavement: we love you and thank you.

TABLE OF CONTENTS

All blank pages are intentional

FOREWORD

I met Alisha in 1994 through my eight-year-old granddaughter while she was standing at her bus stop. My granddaughter was approached by Alisha with a hand-written note. Inside the note was her name and phone number "asking" if her daughter and my granddaughter could ride the bus together. She stated in her note that we were neighbors and asked if I could call her. After I read the note, I agreed to call her. This was my first encounter with Alisha. I didn't know her, and I didn't know where this conversation was going to lead. After speaking with her on the phone, she appeared to be friendly, so I agreed that the girls could ride the bus together. This was the beginning of Alisha's and my friendship. I learned that she was married and had two children. I learned that she worked in a Hospital as a CNA. I got to know her quite well. I can tell you that she one of the most pleasant people I have ever met.

One of the reasons I accepted her friendship was her unselfish character. She had a way of making you feel special. She is one of the most giving and loving individuals that I have ever encountered. She became my best friend, and our friendship grew as time progressed. She would confide in me about some of her deepest, darkest personal matters. She would tell me about things as far back as her childhood. She would tell me about some of the things that she struggled with as a child; things like not being able to keep up in school and at home. I learned about her fear of rejection, and about her fear of not being loved. I didn't know that she was going through so much in her marriage until one day she called me and began to express her emotions and how she felt about her husband. She said that he was having an extramarital affair.

I didn't know that things had gotten so bad between the two of them, to the point where she wanted to kill her husband and take her own life. She was battling depression and suicide all the time. Those silent demons had become so real in her life that she was constantly hearing voices telling her to kill herself. She would call for prayer, but she just couldn't seem to break free from all the turmoil she was facing in her life. Although she went to church every Sunday faithfully and served God, she still didn't have faith power to silence the demons that seemed to be robbing her of her sleep and appetite. These attacks were affecting her physical and emotional health in such a way that she found herself feeling isolated and alone. It wasn't until she fell on her knees and recognized that only something or someone greater than herself could help her. It was then that she decided to rise above herself and to become grounded in the ultimate source of reality. She began to call that source God. Nothing happened until she called on the name of Jesus. It was from that moment that she experienced true deliverance, and from that moment on she was set free from those silent demons of depression, suicide, and grief. She was no longer bound by these spirits, and finally she was set free from all her hurt and pain and all the things that once haunted her past.

In 2011 God blessed her with a wonderful husband named Tyrone - the man of her dreams. He was everything that she had ever wanted in a husband. She knew that God had answered her prayer. He was a Godly man and he loved the Lord. They loved each other dearly. She was the apple of his eye. One of his favorite quotes was "God, You, and Me." Together they started a ministry called "Faith Walk Ministry" The two would often go out and do street ministry. They had a passion for feeding and clothing the homeless. They were a unique couple who shared and did everything together. They were married for five wonderful years. He was diagnosed with throat cancer in 2016, and he fought the battle for seven months until his death in April of 2017 when he went home to be with the Lord.

I believe this book "From Grief to Goodness" will reach a wide range of audiences, those who read this book will realize that her advice comes from her personal experiences. As you read this book, you will take this journey with Alisha., and it will make you think. You may read a chapter and say, "Wow, this really happened to someone?" You may find yourself wondering what you would do if something similar happened to you and what you could have done to prevent this in the first place.

I think Alisha's testimony and the life lessons she shares with her audience in "From Grief to Goodness" is going to give the reader a view into themselves, their families, their friends, their neighbors, and even their co-workers who may have similar problems. I can assure you that you may not find yourself in all these chapters, but you may know someone who experiences issues similar to those outlined in this book, and that they are going to take Alisha's experience and advice and apply it to their life. Because of Alisha's passion and healing, our relationship has grown from being just neighbors and best friends to becoming a Minister and an Evangelist, ministering to the lost.

Minister Janice Weems

1
GRIEF

You may think that this book is all about sadness. Well, let me tell you that you are partly correct. Grief and sorrow have played a huge part of my life. In fact, I never thought I would find myself here, being called to write a book about depression. I have experienced much pain in my life, as have many of you, and I can tell you first-hand how debilitating emotional and mental pain can be. Let's examine pain for a minute.

Pain is the body's way of telling us that something is wrong. It's a warning, so to speak. It tells us we need to change something – to fix something, and fast. But if we focus on the pain we can be deceived into thinking that pain is permanent. We can give in to the idea that our current situation will never be resolved - it will never feel better. The struggle is in remembering that pain – all pain – is only temporary. I am a woman of faith. Together with my husband I have witnessed and ministered to countless people. But the loss of my husband, the love of my life, made me struggle to understand how the pain I felt would ever be lifted. I could not understand why God was allowing us to experience such suffering. Why would He give me such a wonderful gift and then take it away?

My husband Tyrone woke up one morning complaining that his throat was hurting. I could tell something was wrong because he got up every morning at 5 o'clock to spend time with God and go walking in the park with his headset on listening to his favorite radio station. It was a Christian station that featured programs discussing marriage; other programs featured different faith leaders who would preach sermons. Tyrone listened every morning to strengthen his faith and to strengthen our marriage. But this particular morning, Tyrone didn’t get up for his walk, and he didn’t mention his radio programs. Instead, while we were laying in bed, my husband looked at me and a tear fell from his eyes.

I’d never seen him this way. I got close to him and I hugged him tightly. He asked me to pray over him; he said that he didn’t know what it was, but it was like fear just came over him. I began to pray over my husband for healing for his throat and for the pain to leave him. I told him that we needed to make an appointment to go see the doctor and get his throat checked out. We got up and called the doctor's office and were able to make an appointment for the next day. They told us that he would be seeing the ear, nose and throat doctor.

We went in to see the doctor and they wanted to take X-rays of his throat. They put a camera down his throat to get a clear view of what the problem might be. The doctor told us that he wanted to wait on the X-ray to come back before he talked to us. Two days later they gave us a call and told us they had the results and they wanted us to come in to sit down and talk with them. My husband was trusting God; he was still working out every day and listening to the word of God. We asked some of our family and friends to pray for us.

It's important to explain here that up to this point, my husband and I were doing well. Everything was good, and we were very happy. My husband and I were working together in the ministry. We were counseling couples together, and I would go with him to the hospital to visit the sick. My husband was in ministry school at the time, and he was getting ready to be ordained as an Elder at the church. In fact, he would be the only Elder at the church, so it was a great honor for him. He graduated from the school of ministry at Deliverance Mission Christian Church under Pastor Monty Weatherall in 2013, and he received his license as Elder Howard Tyrone Thorpe. So many things were happening with us and our marriage - we were blissful. And now this sickness was trying to take over his body. Nevertheless, we were keeping our faith and keeping our eyes on God.

Tyrone received a phone call the following week from the doctor's office. They told him that they had seen something on the X-ray that didn't look good, and they wanted to perform a biopsy to make sure that it was not cancer. I was sitting down eating dinner when my husband received the phone call. He walked around the dinner table to where I was sitting, gave me a big hug, and told me that he would always love me forever. I responded that I would also love him forever, but that I wanted to know what was going on and what the phone call was about. He told me that it was his doctor on the phone, and that they found something on the X-ray and needed to perform a biopsy to rule out cancer. I took a deep breath and a tear fell from my eye. I remember this moment so vividly – it was Friday evening, June 8, 2013. I said, "My love, our anniversary is in three days. We will be married two years, and we must keep the faith and believe that it is not cancer." My husband didn't speak about the phone call again.

We finished eating, and he told me he had a surprise for me. He said he had made plans for us to get away for the weekend, as an anniversary gift. We went to a log cabin at a beautiful resort that was about two hours outside of Saint Louis, Missouri. We had the best time that weekend, and it felt like our honeymoon all over again. When we got to the resort, we were led to our room and it was the honeymoon suite. I knew that my husband had something big behind the door, because the smile on his face was as wide and bright as it had ever been. He said, "My love, close your eyes." He took my hands and walked me through the door. When I opened my eyes, I saw three dozen roses, three anniversary cards, and seven balloons that said happy anniversary. I was astonished! I said, "Wow, when did you do all of this?" He told me he drove up on Thursday while I was at work on a 12-hour shift.

Tyrone and I liked to play this game where we tried to beat each other at being good. We started this when we first got married. I said, "Honey, you got me this time; I owe you one!" We spent the evening just loving on one another. That evening, we had reservations for a romantic dinner down in the restaurant; it was a five-star establishment. We looked over the menu, and we both ordered steak, a baked potato, and salad. For dessert, we had strawberry cheesecake. While we were sitting there waiting on our food, we reminisced about our first date and how we knew that God had connected our spirits together. I'm telling you, that night we didn't care what happened, we knew that we were in love much deeper that day than the day we got married. During dinner, a man started to walk over to our table. Before I knew it, he started singing, "You are so beautiful to me; you are so beautiful to me; can't you see you're everything I hope for; you're everything I need; you are so beautiful to me." I was just sitting there trying to hold back my tears, but I couldn't. They were tears of joy because I was so happy. My husband said, "My love, I wanted him to sing that song because you are so beautiful to me, and I love you dearly." I got up, walked around the table, sat on his lap, and just kept kissing him. I couldn't stop. But I had a surprise for him, too. I had bought him a necklace that had a cross pendant, and his initials were engraved onto it. He had been eyeing it in the jewelry store for a while, so I knew he would love it. When he opened it, the look on his face was priceless. We were both so overwhelmed with love and joy that by time the food came, we couldn't even eat much so we had to take it to go. The restaurant had a live band that night, so we walked over to the other side of the building where we could enjoy the music.

That Saturday morning, we got up early and went walking. To me it was like hiking; we got so far away from our cabin. I told Tyrone, "We are lost." My honey assured me that we were not lost, and he began to remind me that he had been a boy scout. He also reminded me that he had been in the army: "We lived in the fields! I can find my way back from anywhere!" he exclaimed. And sure enough, he guided us back to safety. For the remainder of that day we hung out around the pool just relaxing and enjoying each other. Around 5 o'clock that evening we got dressed and went out to this restaurant that offered a variety of fish on their menu. They were very well known for their fish and chips. My husband really loved the fish, which was a surprise to me. He worked as a chef, and so he could be very critical when we went out to dinner. He would sometimes say, "My love we could have stayed home and ate." However, it was clear he enjoyed his dinner that night. After we left there, we returned to our cabin. When we got back, I started packing our clothes while my husband took a nap because we would be checking out the following day.

Sunday morning, we got up and got dressed, and then

my husband prayed and read the word of God before we got on the road for our return trip home. I can truly say I had a wonderful weekend with Tyrone celebrating our second anniversary. Our anniversary was actually on June 11th, which was the same day that the doctor had scheduled him for his biopsy. We had to be at Veteran Hospital at 8 o'clock in the morning. We got there at about 7:30 a.m. though, because my husband hated being late for anything. He would always want to get to places 30 to 45 minutes early. Punctuality was one of the many things he helped me with, and we really balanced each other out. My husband wasn't a very patient person and I was, so I would help my husband to develop patience and he would help me work on being on time.

When we got to the hospital the nurses checked us in, and then they came to take my husband for the biopsy. About thirty minutes later, the doctor came into the waiting room to talk with me. I braced myself for the news: he informed me that they did find some cancer on his larynx in his throat. He told me that Tyrone was now in recovery, and that I would be able to see him when he woke up from the anesthesia.

After the doctor left the waiting room, I fell on my knees and began to pray to God. I told Him, here we are celebrating our second anniversary and we receive this news! But I told God that we were going to trust Him, and I wasn't going to focus on the situation or the circumstance - we were going to trust Him, no matter what the medical reports said. A nurse came out to tell me that I could go back in to see my husband. When I got in the room, the doctor came in and told my husband that they found cancer on his voice box in his throat. But he also told us the good news: the tumor they found was as small as a black-eyed pea, and it was at stage one. He said that he thought the best option for treatment was radiation therapy. Once the receptionist had scheduled the first radiation appointment, Tyrone and I looked at each other and I started crying. My husband looked at me and told me, "My love, we are going to be fine because we know GOD got us. We will not look at the situation, but we will keep our eyes on God." I told him that's what I had just been praying for and that is the same thing I saw. Even in our time of greatest trouble, we were on one accord.

My husband said he wanted us to go on a fast while we were going through this. I told him I was fine with that, and asked him how long would we fast for? He told me he would let me know because he was going to pray about it. The nurses came in and began to prepare my husband to check out, but a small complication caused him to have to stay in the hospital overnight. I ended up going home alone, but before I left our Pastor called to check on Elder Tyrone. I told him that they were going to keep him in the hospital overnight, and he told me that he would be come up and pray with Elder Tyrone. The Pastor reminded me God had control of this and I said, "Yes, He does." The next morning, I picked my husband up from the hospital and drove him home.

The doctors did not start his radiation treatment for

about two months. They told us they had to determine the right strength for him and that he had to be sized for a face mask. They finally got everything in place and he started his radiation treatment on August 5, 2013 at 8:00 a.m. He would have to go three times a week. It was truly a blessing because the days that he would go for treatment were the days I would be off work, so I was able to be with him. He was to receive the treatments for 28 days. Around this time, my husband reminded me of the fast he wanted to go on while he was going through the treatments. He told me that he had prayed about it and he wanted to do a 40-day fast. I told him that I was going to fast with him, so all we ate was fruit and vegetables and water and we did not have any juice or sweets. While we fasted, he was also working on writing his sermons. He completed several: "Now you see it, now you don't," "God step in and cancer step out," and "We still on [Psalm 23]." Through everything, he held on to the belief that God truly had us in His hands.

While my husband was undergoing one of his treatments one day, I got a phone call from my oldest sister that our father had a heart attack. She said things didn't look good. I told her only thing I know how to do is to pray. After my husband got done with his treatment that morning, we rushed to the hospital to be with my sisters and brothers in the emergency room. Tyrone and I went in to see my dad, and my husband began to pray over my father's body for healing. He asked my dad whether he believed that God could heal him, and my dad nodded his head yes. After my husband prayed over him I told him I loved him so much, and that we would see him when they got him settled into a room. His nurse told us that they were going to put him in ICU so they could keep a close eye on him. We wanted to wait while they transported him, and she told us it was going to be a while before they moved him, so we could go get something to eat. While we were in the cafeteria with my family eating, we were paged over the intercom to come up to ICU on the fifth floor. As soon as we got up there, the nurse met us at the door and told us things had taken a turn for the worse. She told us they were working on him, and that they were performing CPR right at that moment but he'd had another heart attack. A few minutes later, the doctor came out of the room and he said that they couldn't do anymore; they had been working on him for about 45 minutes and he was not getting any oxygen to his brain. I felt so numb. It was like I was looking around and could see everyone walking and moving but I couldn't hear any sound. Then suddenly it was as if my ears opened up, and I could hear my sisters and my brothers crying. I burst into tears as well, and my husband began to hold me. He reminded me, "You know where he is going because he is a believer and he has accepted God. God said to be absent from the body is to be present with the Lord." As much faith as I had, it was still hard to hear. When you are losing a loved one, you don't want to hear any of that; you just want your loved one to come back. In hindsight, I know my husband was just trying to encourage me and comfort me. We all stayed at the hospital for about two hours, so we would take turns going back to see our dad. My husband and I went back into the room to see my father for the last time before he passed away. It was getting late and my husband was tired from his radiation treatment, so we left the hospital and drove home.

Four days later, we started making the arrangements to put our father to rest. My husband finally completed his last radiation treatment on August 28th.The arrangements were made for our dad's homegoing service on August 30th. A mere two days after a month of radiation therapy, my husband gave the eulogy at my father's service and over 75 people came up and rededicated their lives back to God. I know that was God giving my husband strength because usually after his treatment, he would be in so much pain and feel so weak. But God continued to use him for His glory. A month later the doctor called my husband and told him that they didn't see any more cancer in his throat. He also told him that he would need to come back once a month to get checked out. He told him that he was in remission, and that it was possible to stay in remission for about five years. We were so happy and felt so blessed! After the scariest and saddest summer of our lives together, we were finally getting good news! All we could do was praise and thank God.

Tyrone and I were so happy that he was in remission from the cancer. Every time he went back for his appointments, the doctor said everything was looking good on the X-rays and that he was still in remission. Tyrone was feeling pretty good, which was such an improvement from when he would take his treatments, because they would leave him so weak. During the time he had been going through his radiation, he'd had to stop preaching and so when we would minister at the nursing home, I would go to teach while he was resting and recovering. Now that the doctors had released him, he could resume preaching.

You see, during that month of August of 2013, my husband and I felt a deep calling to leave our church family to do street ministry. We wanted to pray about it before we went to the pastor. We had been fasting for three weeks before we approached him with God's instructions for us. My husband had told me that he really wanted to be in prayer about this because he had been wanting to do this for a while, and he felt like this was the year to do it. He and Pastor Monty Weatherall were very close, and it would break his heart when we left to start our ministry. But we knew that God was calling us for street ministry and nursing home ministry, and we knew that we were going to be a church without walls. My husband also said that we would continue to do our marriage counseling because he felt there was a great need for it. My husband first sat down with the pastor to begin telling him the vision that God had given us. Pastor Weatherall said if that's what God put on our hearts, we had his blessing. He also told Him that he supported my husband and me, and he supported the vision that God gave us. Our Pastor told my husband thathe needed to sit down with both of us together, and so he scheduled a date and time to meet with us. He just wanted to hear from both of us to make sure we were on the same page. He told us it was so hard for him to release Tyrone because they had been together for over 15 years. My husband had been the only Deacon at the church, and then after he went to school for ministry he then became the only Elder at the church. So they had a rich history together.

The two men had met years before; Pastor Weatherall had been conducting a survey and he drove up in his car and stopped to talk to my husband who was standing at the bus stop. Pastor said that he was doing a survey, and he wanted to know if he had time to talk with him. My husband told him that he was waiting on a bus to go to work, and Pastor Monty agreed to take him to work and he would conduct the survey on the way. Little did he know that my husband worked 45 minutes away! But he was a man of his word and he drove him the whole way. During the trip, they began to talk about God, and after that my husband started going to Pastor Monty's church where he ended up giving his life back to Jesus.

My husband was so sold out for Christ, that he would place different scriptures inside newspapers, and he would go to the grocery store and tuck scriptures between items on the shelf. He also told me while he was on the bus, he would be talking to all types of people about God and what He had done for him. He would talk to them about how God had saved him from being on crack cocaine and alcohol. He also witnessed about being saved from cirrhosis of the liver and Hepatitis C. My husband would always tell the people, "Once the Son makes you free, you are free indeed!" Tyrone had been healed from all his diseases.

All that said, my husband was under our pastor for

about 15 years, and so it was hard for him to leave the church that he loved and that he felt had saved him. Pastor Monty gave us a special ceremony at the church. The saints were so happy for us, but sad to see us leave the church. Our pastor blessed us that day and we thanked everyone for the seed we received. My husband said that our pastor was still our overseer, and when he had questions, he would call Pastor Monty for guidance and answers. He would check in with him from time to time to let him know what we were doing and the things that we had planned for the ministry. Pastor Monty Weatherall told us that he wanted us to continue marriage counseling at the church, so we would still be at the church once a week. We would come back to our church home to get rest, study, and hear the word of God every three months.

Tyrone and I became the co-founders of Faith Walk Ministry (FWM). I can truly say starting the ministry was not easy! We had to figure out how to fill the paperwork out to become a non-profit organization and become tax-exempt. There were a variety of ministry costs, but we were believing that God would send people to help us and that is exactly what happened. God put us in contact with so many people who were willing to help us provide care packages, food, and clothing to the needy. We also were blessed by a Christian bookstore that donated over 1,000 bibles to us. When we ran out, we ordered the Bibles from the book store and they gave us a huge discount. We were really doing well with the ministry that God had called us for. In the first year of doing ministry, we fed over 200 people on Christmas and gave away 175 new coats with gloves and scarfs. We fed them Tyrone's famous chili, crackers, peanut butter sandwiches and water. By God's power, at least 70 people gave their life back over to the Lord on that day. My husband had a way of talking to people and telling his testimony that really touched their hearts. He would say, "If God can deliver me from crack, He can save you and deliver you from it too - but only if you believe." Every time he would tell his testimony, people began to fall on their knees crying out asking God to save them, and to deliver them from drugs and prostitution. My husband believed in giving his testimony. He would also give them the Word, but he believed in what the Bible says about winning someone over by your testimony. God kept working in us and through us, and pretty soon FWM was going on three years old. We were so busy! We were doing outreach ministry, hospital visitation, traveling, speaking at different churches, and we would participate in marriage conferences with different organization and different ministries. When we met people, they would ask us where our church is, and we would always tell them our home church is DMCC and our Pastor is Monty Weatherall, but we started an outreach ministry and the name is Faith Walk Ministry.

My husband would always ask the question, how many people would leave the 99 to go get that one lost soul, and before you could reply he would say you were that one. I was that one. Besides doing our ministry, we would travel a lot out of town, and no matter where we went we would always be on a mission for God. Everywhere we found ourselves, my husband and I would do ministry. Our mission was really for the homeless and the lost souls, and for saving and growing marriages. For the broken: that was our mission statement - the same statement that Jesus had. My husband also led a prison ministry, and so he would do bible study with them every other Wednesday. Every fourth Sunday they would come together, and my husband and two other ministers would hold a Sunday service and worship service. Tyrone and I would go and visit a young man who was in prison, and we would spend time with him talking to him about God and the things of God. We would hold a bible study with him. Tyrone was his mentor; they worked together, and he looked at my husband as his spiritual father. He was grateful for our visits, so we would go to visit him every three months and we would put money on his books.

My husband was preaching and ministering so much, and his voice would sometimes sound so weak. Despite how he felt, he would never stop ministering, and he never stopped being a wonderful husband to me. I remember coming home on my birthday one year to find that my king had surprised me with 314 roses that were in vases all throughout my living room. My entire living room was covered up with flowers. I knew every time my husband had a surprise for me; he would have a big smile on his face. So when I walked in the door, the only thing that I could see was the flowers and his big smile. I ran over and jumped into his arms. I thanked him so much! I never had a man give me so many roses. I knew that my marriage was special from the beginning. Our birthdays were five days apart, and we would always go out for one another's birthdays. Birthdays have always been special and important to me, and my husband knew that. In 2015 my husband showed up at my job to surprise me with a new car. He looked at me and told me I couldn't beat him being good because he was just like his Daddy. That's how we would do it in our marriage; we would keep our marriage filled with so much fun.

In 2016, my husband was starting to have really severe pain in his throat again. It started to become so painful; he would be trying to swallow and he couldn't. He didn't have much of an appetite because everything he would try to eat would burn his throat. My husband was not feeling well, but he didn't let that stop him from celebrating our five-year anniversary. We really had a good time that weekend. We drove up to Branson to surprise our special friends in Branson, MO and we were able to fellowship with them at their church. When church service was over with we all went out to dinner, and they were so concerned about Tyrone's throat. Our friend is a doctor and he was asking Tyrone all kinds of questions. They asked us to spend the night with them and we did, and we had a very good visit. We did not know that this would be Tyrone's and his friend's last time hanging out and fellowshipping together. By August, the pain was so unbearable for my husband that we decided he needed to make a doctor's appointment. We went in that following Friday, and they performed additional X-rays.

Right around this time, my husband and I had decided

to take my son and my niece to Florida as a graduation present. We had a good time on the trip celebrating my son's graduation from high school. While we were on the trip, it was just so special, and it seemed like our love was getting stronger and stronger. The whole week we were so connected, and we felt like we did when we first got married. We had no idea that we were getting ready to go through a storm when we got back.

We flew back in to Saint Louis on that Monday, and my husband had a doctor's appointment on Tuesday. The doctor sat down with us and showed us his X-rays. The only thing we could see was big spots on the X-ray. I asked the doctor what that meant, and he told us it didn't look good. I was trying not to get upset, but I said to him, "You told us two months ago when we were here that everything looked good, and now you are telling us that it doesn't look good?" I couldn't understand how the situation could change so fast! My husband told the doctor that he knew something was going on with his throat because he couldn't swallow. He said his throat felt like somebody was cutting him with a knife. I also told him that a knot had appeared on the left side of Tyrone's jaw. They told us that they wanted to schedule him for another biopsy. The doctor said that they would call us within a week to do the biopsy. I demanded, "No we're not going to do it in a week! You guys are going to admit him into the hospital tonight and do it in the morning. You're not the one in pain, my husband is! We want to know what's going on with his throat." I did not even realize I was saying all of this, but I was so frustrated with the doctor for giving us the run around.

They admitted him in the hospital that same day and they performed the biopsy the next morning at about 8:00 a.m. I was waiting patiently, and before my husband went in, we both prayed, and we affirmed that we believed God and we believed that Tyrone was already healed no matter what comes our way. The doctor finally came out and told us exactly what had come our way. She said the biopsy results showed a new cancer in my husband's neck. I dropped my head and began to cry. She asked me if I was okay. I told her, "No, I'm not okay because you guys knew that it was cancer on that screen and you didn't want to tell us". She told me she was so sorry that she had to give me this terrible news, and that they would have to send the biopsy test out to see what stage the cancer was in. I felt like my whole world was in shambles.

The nurse came and got me and took me to where my husband was recovering from the procedure. He woke up and he looked at me; he wanted to know what they said. I told him they said they saw new cancer on the side of his neck. I began to sob as I was telling him what the doctor's report was. I said to my husband, "How could this be happening to us? We were faithful, we loved everybody, and we have helped so many people!" My husband looked at me and said, "My love, all this is in God's hands, and we should not question Him." I know my husband was disappointed, but he was trying to be strong for me. I looked at him and I saw a tear fall from his eyes. He said, "If we can beat it once, we can do it again with the help of the Lord." He told me that we should keep our eyes on Jesus, keep the faith, and believe what God said for his healing. My husband was so strong, and he would encourage me when I would get down – even in his darkest moments. So many people were praying for us; our family and our church family would beseech God for my husband's healing.

I called Pastor Monty to let him know what was going on and he came up to pray with Tyrone. I know my pastor was sad because we were not expecting this type of news. The doctor came in and told us that she had more difficult information to give us. She said that the cancer was soft and looked like it was spreading. This was all taking place the weekend of Thanksgiving in November 2016, and I was off work for four days. I was working at the Veteran Hospital, and when I returned to work, one of the doctors wanted to see me. She is truly one of my favorite doctors, and I love her because she has so much compassion for veterans. She told me that she was sorry to hear about my husband. She began to cry and was very emotional. I started crying also, and I thanked her for her concern about my husband and me. She stated that the reason she wanted to talk to me was to tell me that she went home to share with her husband about Tyrone's diagnosis and asked if I was okay with that. She said her husband was also a doctor and that he specialized in lung and throat cancer. He was willing to give us a second opinion. She told me how special I was as a nurse, and she saw how well I took care of the veterans. She said she noticed how I would go the extra mile, and she wanted to give me the same opportunity I gave to others. She explained that she knew what we had been going through and she wanted to help in any way she could.

I can truly say that all the employees at the hospital were very concerned for my husband, and a lot of them had known Tyrone well because he worked there for over 30 years. They knew that we were so in love; they knew we were so happy to have one another and that we were a blessing to one another. In fact, a few of them thought they knew us too well! After my husband retired, he would come up and have lunch with me, and one of my coworkers saw us walking together holding hands. She thought that I was cheating on my husband with another man and she told us that she began to look at me differently. She said that I couldn't have been a Christian because she thought I was cheating on my husband. One day we were having an event in the cafeteria and my husband came up to the hospital and she went over to say hello. I was just walking into the cafeteria and my husband started to introduce me to her. I said, "Honey she knows me; she comes over to do crafts and recreation therapy with the veterans." She responded, "I am so sorry! I had judged you and your wife because I thought you guys were cheating on your spouses with one another. I thought Alisha was cheating on her husband, but you are her husband!" We all started to laugh. To this day, she still tells that story to the veterans every chance she gets.

My friend the doctor made good on her promise, and we got a phone call from Saint Louis University hospital saying that they were calling from the doctor's office to schedule an appointment for November 30, 2016. We went in and met with the doctor. He was very nice, and he confirmed that he wanted to give us a second opinion. The doctor took a long scope and put it down Tyrone's throat, and when he looked down there he said he did see some red irritation. The first doctor told us that Tyrone's cancer was in stage three, and that's why it was important for us to get a second opinion. This specialist, however, said the cancer was still in stage one, and that he could go forward with surgery to remove the cancer. He explained at that time that the only way he couldn't remove the cancer was if the cancer detached itself from the main arteries of the neck. If that happened, he would have to close Tyrone back up and maybe try to do chemo and radiation to get the rest of the cancer.

My husband and I agreed, and we were believing that the specialist would be able to go in and remove the cancer from his neck. The doctor told us that he would give us a call in a day or two to make arrangements for the surgery. We were sitting in the car getting ready to pull out of the garage at the hospital when the secretary from the doctor's office called and said they had good news for us. She told us that they had scheduled the surgery for the next day, which was December 1, 2016. Everything was moving so fast that we forgot that we had agreed to keep our grandbaby for a week while my daughter was out of town training for her job. My husband and I did not know what we were going to do, because my daughter was already out of town. So, we called up my best friend, to see if she could watch our grandson while we were at the hospital for Tyrone's surgery. She agreed to keep him for us, and she ended up keeping him for four days which was when my daughter returned to pick him up.

We showed up at the hospital on December 1, 2016 and the surgical team prepped him for the surgery. The doctor came in and said he would be in surgery for 12 hours. The doctor explained that if Tyrone's vocal box was damaged when he got inside the throat, they would have to remove it. My husband and I were very concerned, and he told the doctor that he would need his voice box to talk and to preach the word of God. They also told us if that they had to remove the vocal box, they would have to put in a trach. It was a lot to hear and there was much pressure to try to make the right decision. Some of my friends and family were there early that morning to support us, and before my husband went back for surgery, our pastor came to the hospital to pray with us.

That day I was believing that the doctor would be able to remove all the cancer from his neck. We were sitting in the waiting room area and after about four hours the doctor came out. He came out with a look of disappointment on his face - like he was ready to cry. "Alisha, I am so sorry. We were not able to remove all the cancer from his neck." He told us the cancer had started breaking off and was very soft. He said the cancer had detached from the main artery and he said if they kept going they could hurt him and cause damage that could cause him to have strokes for the rest of his life. The doctor told me that he was going to go back in and close him up. He said the good news was that Tyrone was very healthy and once he healed, they could start chemo and radiation on him to remove the rest of the cancer. I was able go to see him in recovery. I saw they had cut my husband from ear to ear, and because of it, Tyrone was extremely sedated. The doctor told us that they would keep him for about a week and then he could go home to heal. He also told us they did a test that determined the cancer was Stage 4-B, and that meant he couldn't go back in to do any more surgeries because if he opened my husband back up the cancer could spread. When my husband woke up, he was in so much pain and I just remember reaching over to give him a big kiss. I simply told him that I loved him so much.

The doctors told him he needed to get up and move around so he could get his strength back. He got up and walked the halls and stopped at every room to stretch out his arm to pray for each patient on the fifth floor. When he made it back to his room, he said to me, "Honey I am so tired." I said, "You have ministered to so many people that it has drained your strength." Twenty minutes after we returned to the room, the doctor came in to explain the type of cancer he had and what our options were. He told us we could work on his recovery and then look into doing chemo, or we could do chemo first, and then three doses of radiation if he was a candidate. Since he had previously had radiation treatment on his neck, and the doctors do not like to repeat it in the same area, we had a lot to consider. Tyrone remained in the hospital for three days before being released to go home.

We left the hospital and stopped at the pharmacy to pick up his medicine. While we were waiting for his medicine, he started sweating and looking confused. I got him to the car, got him home and then got him inside the house. I started taking his temperature, blood pressure, and I did an assessment of his neck to make sure the drainage was okay. When I looked at the drainage, I saw a knot had appeared on his neck about the size of a quarter. I immediately called the doctor who was on call at the hospital for the weekend with my concerns. He told me not to worry because it could be old blood where the drainage was, and it would sometimes swell after surgery. I stated to the doctor that he was also spiking a fever, and he told me if it reached 102 to bring him back to the hospital. That night as we got ready to lay down, I checked his temperature and the fever was still running around 101 at that time. I called the doctor again and told them the knot had not gone down and that blood was coming from the drainage. He told me to take a picture of it and send it to him. He told me to keep an eye on it and let him know if there were any other changes in his condition. At 4:00 a.m., God woke me up and told me to check on my husband. When I woke up, Tyrone was up trying to walk to the bathroom and I could see that he appeared confused; he was sweating, shivering, and stumbling. He never made it to the bathroom, I sat him down on the side of the bed and got the urinal for him to use. After he was done using the urinal, I immediately checked his temperature and at that time it was 106.5. I called the ambulance and told them my husband had a temperature of 106.5 and I needed assistance. They told me an ambulance would be sent out to our home immediately and to leave the door open so they can come right in. I called the doctor to let them know we were on our way back to the emergency room.

Right after I got off the phone, Tyrone started to pass out. His eyes were rolling around in his head, and he was foaming at the mouth as if he was having a seizure. I began to scream out, begging for someone to come and help us. I stopped however, because I realized I needed to remain calm because he needed me to help him, and I couldn't if I panicked. God gave me the strength to get him on his side because he was starting to slide off the bed. I realized that what my husband needed at that time was a nurse and not a wife, and my nursing skills kicked in. I started shaking him to keep him alert and awake and to get a response from him. By this time, the ambulance had arrived, and they came in and started assessing his condition and asking questions. I told them this was not the time to ask questions, that we needed to get him to the hospital immediately because he was a cancer patient who had surgery on the left side of his neck and may have an infection. They put him in the ambulance and wanted to take him to the nearest hospital, but I begged and pleaded with them to take him to SLU Hospital where he was under the treatment of a doctor on staff. They finally agreed to take him to SLU, and I stayed behind to lock up the house and get all the information they would need at the hospital.

When I got to the hospital I was very emotional. I was anxious to see my husband and find out his status. The nurse who was working with my husband came out to meet me and update me on his status. He told me that they had been working on Tyrone for 45 minutes trying to get his fever down. They put him on a cooling bed to try to break the fever and had also given him antibiotics, but nothing seemed to be working. A call had been made to the doctor and he was on his way to the hospital. When Tyrone saw me, he began to say, "Honey, I am sorry. Please just let me go home." He said he was tired and his body had been through so much. I said, "I know honey, but we are fighters. God's got us, and it is not time for you to go home." Right after that, the doctor came in; they immediately cut open the incision to drain the infection from his neck. Tyrone's brother who is also a pastor made it to the hospital and he began to witness to Tyrone to keep him focused and that seemed to calm him down. He stopped talking about dying and started saying yes, he wanted to live to stay here with his wife because we still had work to do. He said that was the devil talking to him trying to get him to give up. They got his fever down and he remained in the hospital in ICU for three days.

I called his only daughter to let her know what was happening. I told her it would be best for her to come in town to see her dad as soon as she could. She decided to immediately fly in from Tampa, Florida to be at her dad's side. I went home to allow her to spend time alone with her dad, so they could talk. She spent the day and all night at the hospital at her dad's bedside. While she was there, the doctor came in and told us the plan was to finish the antibiotic treatment and then do the first round of chemo, before he left the hospital. He was released from the hospital and the following week, he started his treatments for chemo. He received six chemo treatments, and then they told us they would do an X-ray to see if the cancer was shrinking. While we were in the office waiting on the test results, the doctor came to talk with us. He said, "I have good news and bad news; which one do you want to hear first?" My husband said, "Let me hear the good news first." The doctor said that the good news was that they have a treatment called Keytruda, which is an immunotherapy drug that they could try that would help build up his immune system and would go search for the cancer and kill the cancer cells. He said the bad news was that the type of cancer my husband had was very fast growing and aggressive. He also informed us that day that they would no longer continue the chemo treatments because they were not working. The plan was to start the Keytruda treatment in two weeks; he would have this treatment every three weeks instead of the daily chemo treatments.

While we were waiting to start the treatment over the weekend, Tyrone became very weak and was having trouble breathing. I took him back to the emergency room, and the doctor met us there and reminded us that because of the cancer and where it was in his neck, it could start affecting his breathing. He asked Tyrone if he would allow him to put the trach in to help open his airway, which would give him comfort and help with his breathing. He also talked to Tyrone about his weight; he was losing a lot of weight and the doctor was concerned that he wasn't getting the proper amount of nutrients since he could not swallow. They decided that he would put in a G-tube and the trach during the same procedure. They admitted him to the hospital and completed both procedures. The dietician talked with us about his tube feeding and the training we would need before he could be released from the hospital. My husband would say, "Alisha, you are not a nurse right now, you are on leave taking care of your wonderful husband." He wanted me to listen to them and learn to do it their way.

The following week they started him on the Keytruda treatment, however he started to decline physically. The doctor wanted to stop the treatment and start radiation to try and shrink the tumor. But then they noticed that the radiation was burning him so badly that the wound began to open and spread. By now it was around Christmas and his daughter and her family came back into town to spend the holidays with us. My husband was able to cook Christmas dinner. Even though he was weak, he insisted on making his famous turkey and sides. Everything was delicious! That was one of the best Christmases ever, and it was one we will never forget. We had family and friends come over on Christmas Eve, and one of my friends brought her three beautiful and talented daughters to sing a song for Tyrone that we knew would lift his spirits. She had her four sons sing a song for him as well. It was so amazing and beautiful, and we can truly say we had praise and worship on that day. My daughter and son-in-law were so touched by the teaching, the praising, and the love that was shown to Tyrone that day. When my son-in-law returned home, he called and said he had been watching the video that was recorded. He said he had received so much that day that it made him look back over his own life and made him want to get closer to God.

On his birthday the following month, my husband got up and called his niece and invited her and her family to come over to have breakfast with him. Even though he was not able to eat, he really enjoyed cooking for others, and that is what he wanted to do that day. He wanted me to dance with him, and he asked his niece to record us. The cancer had become so aggressive that it was now eating away his neck, to the point that the trach came out and I could not put it back in. I called my girlfriend and she came to the house to drive us to the hospital. When we got to the hospital, the doctor came in with about six staff members to help position Tyrone, so they could put the trach back in. In the middle of this procedure, Tyrone took a turn for the worse. The doctor talked to me and told me that because my husband was so weak, he wasn't a good candidate for any more radiation because it was not working. I was trying to be strong and not cry in front of my husband, so I immediately stepped out of the room and began to pray and ask God to give me the strength to deal with the news we had just received.

Right after that, my phone rang, and it was our close friends from Branson. The husband was a retired doctor, and they were calling to check on us. He could tell I was crying and upset, and I began to tell him everything the doctor had just discussed with us. He told me, "Alisha, keep trusting God and know that God's will, will be done." Tyrone and I were very close to him and his wife. In fact, he'd had a triple by-pass on the same day Tyrone had his surgery, so we were not able to be there physically for them and they were not able to be here for us, but we were with each other spiritually. A week later, he came down with his lovely wife to visit Tyrone in the hospital, and that was the last time they saw each other. Tyrone was happy to see them, and the doctor was happy and emotional while he was visiting. While they were visiting together, his wife and I went to lunch to talk, and she prayed with me and comforted me.

Tyrone never improved after that and he came home on hospice. I took care of him until he passed away a month later. Now I was faced with how to go from grief to goodness.

The time I spent with Tyrone during our marriage afforded me so many rich memories, so much happiness, and showed me just how much love God had for me to bless me with a husband who adored me. But now, at the end of our journey together, my wonderful husband was gone, and my faith hadn't seemed to be enough to keep him here. Still, I couldn't understand why my husband had to leave!

Grief can grip you. It is emotional pain that can eat away at your faith in the same way that cancer had affected Tyrone. Unless we are prepared to deal with grief with the Truth of the Word of God, grief can overcome us. We must remember who God is to us in our time of grief.

These scriptures can help us cling to God when we are grieved, instead of clinging to our sadness alone:

Matthew 5:4

Blessed are those who mourn, for they will be comforted.

Revelation 21:4

He will wipe away every tear from their eyes. There will be no more death or mourning or crying or pain, for the old order of things has passed away.

Psalm 34:18

The Lord is close to the brokenhearted and saves those who are crushed in spirit.

Psalm 147:3

He heals the brokenhearted and binds up their wounds.

If we can hold on to these truths, we can be set free from the grips of grief. But we must be equipped with the Word first. You see, the loss of my husband was only the culmination of my heartbreak. I had experienced a life full of suffering and pain before Tyrone came and showed me what God had truly intended for me. Unfortunately, that meant that I had been used to dealing with grief in many unhealthy ways. It was only God's mercy and grace that kept me during those times.

Reflections

Questions

1. We've all had to or will survive loss. Who are some important people or a person you've loss?

2. How did this person/people or even things add value to your life?

3. Legacy is the inheritance that we leave for someone else, generations after us. Not so much monetarily, but what is legacy of those that you lost? What will be your legacy?

Reflections

Reflections

Reflections

Reflections

2
GRACE

Looking back over much of my life, there were many times where it was hard to see God working. Despite my faith, the trials and tribulations in my life sometimes made it difficult to remember the sufficiency of God's grace. My struggles didn't begin when I lost my husband. They began much earlier in my life.

I was born in St. Louis, MO. My parents were married in 1964 and had six children: three boys and three girls. I was the second oldest and the middle girl. Dad drove for the local bus company, and my mom worked two custodial jobs, one at a bank and one at a children's group home. My dad was also a pastor, and we went to church every Sunday and to Bible study on Wednesdays. I was baptized by my dad when I was five years old. During my childhood, I thought of us as being poor. We grew up eating a lot of beans and rice, and we made sandwiches that did not have any meat. My mother would cook liver and gravy a lot because it was inexpensive. When we went to school, we would have to wear the same clothes for two days; only on the third day could we put on a different outfit.

On the weekends, we would get a treat for dinner and it would usually be fried rice from the local Chinese restaurant. I really looked forward to the weekends because I also looked forward to going to my grandmother's house on my Dad's side. I found that when I was at my grandmother's house I never wanted to leave to go back home. One weekend when I was nine years old, I asked her if I could just live with her because I did not want to go back home. She said that she would have to talk it over with my parents, and I immediately jumped up and gave her a big hug and a kiss. I was so excited and happy, and she hadn't even asked my parents. I wanted to stay with her because all eight of us lived in a three-bedroom house, and my parents shared a bedroom. The three boys shared a room and a bed, and the three girls shared a room and a bed. When I was at my grandmother's house I had a room and bed all to myself, and it was wonderful. My grandmother phoned my mom and asked her if I could stay; she explained that I had asked and that I really wanted to stay. My mother immediately agreed and said that it sounded like a good idea. She told my grandmother that she would help with my care, and she signed over her parental rights to my grandmother so she could raise me. My parents paid child support for my clothes and food. My grandmother enrolled me in the local elementary school and I started attending. I really enjoyed living with my grandmother and at the ages of nine and ten; I would go to the store for her and she would give me chores and responsibilities. Even while living with my grandmother, I would go over to my parents' home to visit with my siblings. However, my absence put a strain on our relationship, and I could see that it was different now that we no longer lived in the same house.

I remember finishing my eighth-grade year, and I was looking forward to going to high school. During that summer, my grandmother signed me up to go to modeling school. I think it was because I was such a tomboy at the time, and she wanted me to act more like a young lady. That was a wonderful experience, and I began to see myself as a young lady. I began to wear make-up and dresses, and that program really helped my self-confidence. It taught me how to enhance my natural beauty. I also got a chance to go to Chicago that summer to visit with my grandfather. He and my grandmother were still married but had been separated for several years.

While in Chicago, I got a chance to meet and hang out with cousins whom I had never met before. One day we went to the store, and when we came out a group of gang members took my tennis shoes. They said I had to give them my shoes because they represented another gang. I didn't know anything about that; I only knew that my grandfather had just bought those shoes for me. I ran home crying and stated that I had been robbed by some female gang members. I told my grandfather I wanted to go back home and that I didn't want to be in Chicago because it was a bad place. The next day he put me on the Greyhound bus, and I went back to my grandmother in St. Louis.

In the fall of 1985, I started high school - and I started liking boys. I found myself doing my homework but easily losing my focus. My freshman year was very challenging for me. We had a lot more homework than in elementary and I was also running track. I made it through my freshman and sophomore years, and then I met the guy who would become my first husband. We started dating even though he was five years older than I was. My grandmother told me that I was changing; she was noticing that I would not come straight home from school like I used to. I tried to tell her that I was with my girlfriend, but she told me that was not true. She called my girlfriend's mother to check and see if I was there and she told her no, I had not been to their house. My grandmother demanded that I tell her the truth. I broke down and told her the truth: I had been dating an older guy and that is where I was going after school. He was a security guard who worked right across the street from my school. Once I told my grandmother the truth about where I had been and who I was with, she called his job and stated to them that he was dating me and that I was a minor. She told them that if they did not do anything to stop it, she was going to call the police and press charges. She did that to frighten him into leaving me alone. It worked for a year.

He left St. Louis and joined the US Army; he was

stationed in Texas. When I turned 18, I received a letter from him telling me that he wanted to apologize to my grandmother for causing problems between us. He also stated that he had always loved me and wanted to marry me; he said that he had been waiting until I turned 18 to approach me again because it would then be legal. I wrote him back and told him yes, I would marry him. Right after that I told my grandmother that he wanted to marry me. She said if I left to go be with him I was not welcome to come back. She said he didn't love me and I was just a child to him. Two weeks later, I received the plane ticket and flew to Killeen, Texas despite my grandmother's advice. I got to Texas on a Friday and we were married the next Monday. I was a virgin when we got married and on the day of our wedding, we had the ceremony and went back home to celebrate. He asked me what I had been doing while we were apart, and I told him I had been hanging out with friends and that one of them was my best friend who happened to be male. I didn't see it coming, but the nextthing I knew I was smacked in the face and knocked down. He immediately picked me up and he said that he was sorry, but that he was upset when I said my best friend was a male. This was the beginning of a very abusive relationship that lasted just one year but felt much longer. Right after that incident, he was shipped off for three weeks for military duty. While he was away, I completed my junior year of high school. I realized I was pregnant a month after getting married, and right after I had our little girl was the second time he hit me. I had a part-time job at a local fast food restaurant, and he would come in and wait on me to get off. He claimed I was flirting and carrying on with my male co-workers. He was jealous, insecure and verbally abusive.

Not long after that he was dishonorably discharged from the Army, and he started working as a cab driver. He also started using cocaine. When he would come home, he would be angry, hollering that I should have his food ready when he walked through the door. One day when I told him his dinner was ready and that it was in the oven, he really flew out of control. As I bent over to get his dinner out of the oven, he started pulling my hair and hitting me and kicking me in my ribs. I put my arm up to protect my face but, he beat me in the head, back and ribs. After beating me, he tore my clothes off and raped me. All the time he was doing this, our baby girl was laying in her crib in the same room. He left the house, and when he was finally done I cleaned myself up, took care of my baby, and then cried myself to sleep. The next day when he went to work, I packed my stuff up and shipped it home. I had to quit my job and I hid out for two weeks with some military friends who gave me the rest of the money I needed to fly my daughter and me home. Ironically, when we got back to St. Louis, we stayed with his mother because I could not go back to my grandmother's house who warned me before I left to go be with him. His mother didn't let him know that we were staying with her. I stayed with her until I got a job and saved enough money to get us a small apartment at the age of twenty. I worked hard to take care of my baby girl and to save money, so I could get a divorce.

At the age of twenty-one, I was a divorced and single mother of a two-year-old girl. I was working full-time as a manager at a fast food restaurant and was back in school taking college courses to earn my Associate's degree in Early Childhood Education. I saved enough money for a down payment to purchase my first home. That was a great achievement for me as a single mother. My relationship with my grandmother was starting to get close again. I would go over to visit her, and she was happy to see me and her great-granddaughter. I got back into church and my life was finally beginning to get better. I rededicated my life back to the Lord and was rebaptized. I found myself working in the Outreach Ministry in the church, and I was happy because I was helping other people. A year after becoming a member, I was nominated to be president of the ministry; that was a proud moment, and it felt good being of service. My daughter was continuing to grow and was involved in the church. She soon started school and was at the top of her class.

I was sitting in my car on the day of my daughter Davida's graduation from her preschool class. Her teacher called me to ask if Davida could be Valedictorian of her class. I told the teacher yes, we would accept the recognition. So, at the graduation they had my daughter stand up and read. To my astonishment, she stood and read from the piece of paper: "We can do all things through Christ that strengthens us, and what we learned in pre-kindergarten we will take it with us to kindergarten." We thought she was done speaking but she continued, "With the help of the Lord on our side, if God is for us who can be against us." The whole class stood up and just clapped. I stood up with so much pride and emotion; I couldn't believe my five-year-old could read all that! My daughter was truly smart, and I always say that she was gifted by God for the things she was saying and doing, and she loved to read. That was such a big success for me and my daughter, and it also reminded us that we must believe when we pray. I went through a lot as a single mother and I felt blessed that she was turning out to be a good girl. I thanked the teacher about two or three times for even selecting Davida to stand before the class. Her teacher was a believer and she spoke about God every chance she got. My daughter would come home all the time talking about the Bible that her teacher would read to the kids; she would read the Bible to them during nap time and it would put them to sleep. That was such a blessing because when my daughter would come home, she would remember the scriptures that had been read to her, and she would want me to read them to her again when it was time for bed. Those teachings stayed with Davida as she grew up and became a young lady. Reading and studying the Bible was something that she and I would do all the time. I would pray with her every night and she was always looking forward to it.

Even so, life as a single mother was still very difficult. I had to begin to rely on the help of my grandmother. As a fast food manager, I had to open the restaurant, meaning I would have to be at work at 4:00 a.m. During the week, I would have to take a cab to drop off my daughter at the daycare. From the daycare, she would go to school in the morning, and on Friday night she would go over to stay with her grandmother for the weekends. I would bring her home Sundays after church. But as I was working on the weekends I would find myself getting off work, going home to change my clothes, and hanging out with my girlfriends at the local nightclubs. Instead of taking advantage of opportunities to spend time with my daughter, I would let her stay at her grandmother's while I went out. I felt myself getting off track and doing things that I knew were not of God. I would go to the nightclub on Saturday nights and then go to Sunday School and Church on Sunday mornings. I would have to arrive at church for Sunday School at 8 o'clock in morning, but I would not come in from the nightclub until about 6 o'clock in the morning. I was at a Baptist church, and before the preacher started his sermon he would start in about sin. The preacher would always say God knows what you're doing; you party on Saturday and you come to the house of the Lord on Sunday like you haven't done anything. I would say, "why is the preacher always talking about me?" He would make me feel convicted every time. It seemed as though, every time I would go to church, the preacher would preach about sin and hell. It felt like he had been watching me and knew about my secret life of partying. I would be so embarrassed. But I knew that God was everywhere at the same time. God knew that I'd been at the nightclub, and it would convict me forever more. I remembered Romans 7:15-20:

For what I am doing, I do not understand. For what I will to do that I do not practice; but what I hate, that I do. If, then, I do what I will not to do, I agree with the Law that it is good. But now, it is no longer I who do it, but sin that dwells in me. For I know that in me (that is, in my flesh) nothing good dwells; for to will is present with me, but how to perform what is good I do not find. For the good that I will to do, I do not do; but the evil I will not to do, that I practice. Now if I do what I will not to do, it is no longer I who do it, but sin that dwells in me.

Because I knew what the Word said it was not me doing it, but the sin in me, I kept repenting to God every time I would go out to the nightclub. Then, when I would go back to church, I would be praying that Pastor Jimmy wouldn't preach or talk about sin. Nevertheless, Pastor Jimmy would tell stories about nightclubs and about the things that go on inside of them, and I would begin to look at him and say, "How did he know about all that stuff in the nightclub?" Every single time, it would make me think that he was talking about me or that he was there at the nightclub when I was there. But that was the guilt that I was feeling about what I was doing, I was just justifying why he was preaching so much about sin.

I found myself drifting away from God. I started working a second job at a local hospital. I had worked at the fast food restaurant for seven years, and I began to get burnt out working early in the morning at the restaurant and going to the hospital in the evening. It didn't give me a lot of time with my daughter, and I found myself drifting away from her because of all the hours I worked. When I would pick up my daughter from my grandmother's house, I noticed that she wouldn't call me mommy or mama anymore; instead she would accidentally call me Granny. I was thinking that it must have been confusing to her, because she would be with her grandmother more than she was with me. I did not want things to go the way they did when I was a kid, where my grandmother raised me and not my mother. I didn't want that to happen to my daughter. I had to decide not to let my grandmother raise her. I wanted to raise my daughter, so I realized I had to let one of the jobs go so I could spend more time with her. This decision was one of the most important decisions I could have made. Soon I was only working one job, spending more time with my daughter, and doing more with her. I stopped going out to the nightclubs; I was going to church and bible study regularly and reconnected with God. I just remembered what the word says in Proverbs 22:6: "Train up a child in the way he should go: and when he is old he will not depart from it."

I was working, and I was classified as part-time, but I was working full-time hours for Cardinal Glennon Hospital. My job titles were dietary food service and catering. I really loved my job, but the pay was low and there were no benefits because I was considered part-time. One Friday around noon, I received a call from a different hospital which was a rehabilitation hospital. I was being offered an interview for a position at that hospital as a supervisor. A lady by the name of Judy was calling me, asking whether I was still interested in the job I had applied for previously. I told her, "Yes, yes, I am!" Immediately after I hung up the phone, I started screaming "Thank you Jesus!" The three other employees who were in the room when I got the phone call looked at me real funny and one employee asked me, "Are you okay?" I told him, "Yes, I just got so excited because I have been waiting for this phone call for over a month!" I was so happy, and I went back on the floor where I had been working. I was just smiling all day; the smile was so big you couldn't even erase it off my face. I just worked and talked to God all day; I began to Thank him for all the things he was doing in my life: "Thank you God for giving me more money; thank you for a new position; thank you because now I will have benefits for me and my daughter; thank you Lord that I will have money in my bank account, thank you that I will have the money to give my tithes and offerings..." I was so happy that you could not tell me anything. My faith was so big, and I was speaking things as though they had already happened. I was claiming my position even though I hadn't even had the interview yet.

That night when I got off work, I went home to celebrate and tell my daughter all about it. She just looked at me and said, "Mommy, you look so happy." She didn't understand how much this was going to mean to our future. The next day I took her out to celebrate and we had a great time. On Sunday, it seemed like I was the first person to get to the church. I went in and was just praising the Lord like that was my last day here on earth. I was just thanking God with my hands raised high and a big tear fell from my eyes and I just kept saying, "Thank you, God…thank you, God." I felt deep down that I had the position and that it had my name written all over it. On Monday morning, I had to be at the interview at 9:00 a.m. During the interview, she asked me to tell her a little bit about myself. I stated to her that I was a single and divorced mother and that for my first job, I had worked at fast food restaurants. I told her that I started working at the age of 16, and that I became a crew leader which is a position where you would oversee a shift of employees. I explained that I eventually became a supervisor and I would be required to open and close the restaurant. She told me the position would be full-time with benefits and the starting pay would be $24.000 a year. The job duties would be supervising a staff consisting of ten employees, processing payroll, and submitting the end-of-the-month reports. I would supervise the kitchen and the restaurant that the hospital staff used as well. I was so happy, all the tasks seemed like a lot of work, but I didn't care. I would be increase my salary from $10,000 to $24,000 a year. That was a huge increase for me. I thanked her for the interview and the opportunity, and then I asked her what day I could start work. She laughed and said she had three other people to interview and once she had completed her interviews, she would call within a week. Now keep in mind, I had the interview that Monday, and on Thursday, she called me to let me know that she had decided. She told me she felt I was the right person for the job and offered me the position. She asked me if I would accept the job and I told her yes, I would. I asked to give my current employer a two-week notice, and she agreed with my request. I put in my two weeks' notice with my current employer and they all said they were sad to see me leave. On my last day of work, they gave me a surprise going away party. I was not aware that they had planned anything, and they really surprised me. They began to give me hugs and gifts, and they told me how wonderful of an employee I had been. It finally seemed as though all my years of struggle and bad decisions were being reversed. I could finally take care of my daughter. I had reconnected with God, and I just knew it was Him granting me all these blessings. Even though I had experienced struggling with sin and had been hurt at the hands of an abusive husband, God was turning things around for me. This surely was His grace; it was evidence of His unmerited favor over my life.

I started my new job. I was excited when I arrived there on my first day. I met my employees for the first time and they were nice and respectful. Some of them were older than I was, but they looked at me as their supervisor and I felt I was doing well. My 90-day probationary period was coming up, and my supervisor called to tell me that she needed to talk with me immediately and that it was very important. She did not state to me on the phone that my 90-day probationary period was coming up, nor did she tell me what she needed to talk to me about. Immediately I hung the phone up and my heart started beating so fast. Fear came over me, and I did not know where it came from. That was the fear of Satan. John 10:10 says that the devil comes to kill, steal and destroy and he has nothing good for us. But God says, "I come to bring you life."
Immediately I started praying and saying, "God whatever this

feeling is, please take it away from me. This meeting is going to be all positive, and Lord I thank you for opening doors no man can close and closing doors no man can open. Help my faith, let my eyes and ears be open to hear only your voice and not the enemy's voice." I went upstairs to meet with my supervisor. Her door was open, and she gave me a welcoming smile. She told me she wanted to go over my 90-day performance evaluation. I said to myself, "Whew! I didn't know what she wanted to see me about!" As I sat down, she then gave me an envelope with my name on it. I started to put it in my lab jacket and she instructed me to go on and open it now. Inside was a bonus check for $400! She explained that we had exceeded our quota for the quarter and we were receiving a bonus. I had only been employed there for two months so that was a great accomplishment. She went on to tell me that I would also receive a $2.00 per hour raise.

Then she went over my performance evaluation and she said I had outstanding performance. She was very pleased with how I performed my duties, and she was grateful to be working with me. I stated to her that I felt blessed to be working with the company. As I began to walk out of her office, she asked me if I knew of a cook who was looking for employment? She stated the head cook was resigning, and they were looking for someone to fill the position. I told her that yes, my brother was looking for a job and he had just been released from prison three months ago. I told her he was on house arrest looking for a job. I began to thank God, because I realized this was an opportunity for my brother to do right and get back on his feet. She told me I needed to have him complete an application and she would interview him. She interviewed him, and two weeks later he was hired as the head cook. He truly was a good cook and everyone on the job loved him. He felt good making money and giving back. Even though I was his supervisor, we had boundaries at work. He would respect me as his supervisor and I would respect him as an employee.

Right after that, I got a phone call from an old friend who I had not talked to in about six months. She told me she was having a birthday party and she wanted to invite me. She asked me if I would come, and I was so happy to celebrate her birthday with her. I told her I had something to celebrate as well. I told her about my full-time job as a supervisor and that I would love to come out to her party. Her birthday party was at a nightclub, and I had not gone out in a couple of years. I got to the nightclub and felt a little uncomfortable, but I said it was not about me, it was about celebrating my girlfriend's birthday. I noticed when I walked into the room that a gentleman was sitting with another young lady over on the other side of table from where I was sitting. He kept staring at me, and I was so confused because I was wondering why this guy was looking at me when he was sitting with his wife, or so I assumed. He got up from the table and came over and asked me if I would dance with him. I told him thank you but no thank you, and then he offered to buy me a drink and I told him I was drinking water. He sat there and talked with me a while and then he went back to his table. I started socializing with my girlfriend and her guests. We were laughing and talking and having a good time. I was only there for about an hour when I started getting sleepy, and I told my girlfriend I was going to leave and thanked her for inviting me to the party.

Two weeks later, I got a phone call from my girlfriend, and she told me the guy that was talking to me at her party was her brother. She told me he was really interested in me. I asked her if he was in relationship because the last time I saw him, he was with a female. She stated that the lady was his co-worker and friend and that they "hung out together sometimes." This sounded suspicious to me, but when she asked me if it was okay to give him my phone number, I said yes. She gave him my phone number and a week later, he called me. We began to talk. He shared with me that he was a local truck driver, and I told him about my supervisory position. We began to date and around our two-month anniversary, he asked me to marry him. I accepted his proposal. A week later, I woke up to go to work and I was feeling sick. I was throwing up and sick to my stomach. I couldn't eat anything, and I couldn't even hold down water. My daughter woke up and she began to put cold, wet towels on my face. My fiancé told me I needed to go to the hospital because I had really been sleeping a lot. I made an appointment to go to the doctor. My appointment was a week later, and the doctor took a pregnancy test and told me that I was four weeks pregnant. I was so surprised! My daughter was six years old at the time, and now I would be having another child! My fiancé was waiting impatiently in the waiting room, and when I went out there, he had a big smile on his face.

Tears were rolling down my eyes and he asked, "What's wrong, honey? Is everything ok?" I told him that I was not sad; I was happy and sad at the same time! I told him I was pregnant. He was so excited that he started swinging me around and thanking everyone in the doctor's office. I now had this little baby in my belly that I already started to care about. It was like I was starting over again since it had been almost seven years since I had been pregnant. My daughter was the only child in my life, and all this was going to be new.

When I went back to work I told my supervisor that I was pregnant. She congratulated me and told me that I would have maternity leave, and that if I was not feeling well or needed to go home, please let her know. She was very supportive to me. She and all my employees gave me a surprise baby shower, and it was nice. I really appreciated all the beautiful gifts.

My fiancé and I sat down and discussed our relationship. He told me he wanted to move in with me. He was living in a duplex that he was renting in Illinois, and I was living in the home I was buying in Missouri. I told him before we could move in together, we needed to be married. He wanted to wait until about a year after the baby was born to get married. I told him I wanted to get married before the baby was born so that it would have his last name. I also told him I would like him to attend counseling with me, and the pastor of my church would be the facilitator. He looked at me with a strange look on his face. We had been together for some time now, and he had only gone to church with me four or five times during our relationship because he was a truck driver and would be gone a lot. But immediately after I found out I was pregnant, I wanted to do some marriage counseling because I knew that we would need it with this new baby on the way. He looked at me and stated that we did not need counseling at all and that we could just get married without counseling. However, I insisted.

Keep in mind the red flags were coming up even before we got married. As we were preparing for our first counseling session, my pastor first told us it was important to not be unequally yoked. 2 Corinthians 6:14 tells us, "Do not be yoked together with unbelievers." When my pastor reminded us of this, my fiancé jumped up and said, "What are you trying to say? I believe in God, what are you trying to say about me?" I knew then that everything the pastor would say to him, he would find offensive. The pastor stated to us that he wanted to make sure of the foundational principles in the first counseling session. He explained that he would go over salvation with both of us and ask us if we were believers. My fiancé apologized and said, "OK. Thank you. I'm so sorry I thought you were pointing at me. Yes, I am a believer; I have accepted Jesus as my Lord and Savior." Once we got past that everything was going well, and the sessions we were doing began to improve.

While we were going to marriage counseling, I began to show. I was a couple months pregnant by this time, and everything was still going well with my job and with our wedding plans. My fiancé and I went to lunch one Saturday morning; he wanted to go over the details about moving in with me. We both agreed to only have one home, so he would be moving in with me and everything was settled, or so I thought. My pastor called me to say that he had been praying for me, and that he noticed that my fiancé had not been joining me at church so that he could become a member. I told him my fiancé was often working on the weekends, and that he would usually be home only during the week, so it was hard to come to church. You know how it is; we try to make all kinds of excuses. But my pastor was able to see things that I couldn't see. He said he would continue to pray for our marriage I thanked the pastor for praying and for recognizing what might have been an issue. Seven months later we were married.

Immediately after my son was born, my husband's intentions changed. He now wanted to talk about moving me and the kids to Illinois rather than him coming to live in my home in Missouri. He told me that he wanted to take this new position that would bring more money into the home, but it would cause him to be gone more. It sounded good. I think we tend to look only at getting more money, but we don't always look at the consequences behind it. He said that he was taking this job for more money. This would keep him away from the home and from his family. I had to have help raising my son. My mother-in-law was helping, and my husband would pay her to babysit while I was at work. I was still working as a supervisor and my husband started his new job and was gone through the week; he would only come home on the weekends. The kids would be happy to see their Dad and so would I, but working a full-time job and taking care of kids is difficult. Sometimes I wouldn't get into bed after until 10 o'clock at night. I spent my evenings feeding my children and going over their homework. I would pray with them and talk with them about how their day went. I felt myself getting so tired on the days I would go to work; it would be so unbearable and sometimes I could hardly stay awake.

My boss noticed that I would be overworked from time to time, and she asked me if everything was going okay. I told her that the last three years of my marriage, I felt like I was all alone and that I was raising my kids by myself. She was asking me all these questions at my weakest point; I just needed to vent, and it seemed like I could do that with her. I went on talking about my husband and how he took a full-time job and it forced me to be there with the kids by myself, so I had to do everything. I felt like she was so concerned. She had my full attention; she was telling me if I ever needed some extra time off to just let her know and she would do all she could to help me. I thanked her very much and assured her that I would still do my part as a supervisor. I made sure she knew that I would not slack in my job, she said she appreciated me saying that.

I returned to my office. I just felt like my world was tumbling down; I was really stressed and overwhelmed. It seemed like things were falling apart again. When my husband would come home on the weekends we would try to sit down and have family time together, but he was a self-employed truck driver. This meant he had to keep up with lots of paperwork, and that was how he needed to spend his Saturday mornings. It didn't allow us to do a lot together as a family. Other times when he would come home, he wouldn't be in a mood to do anything with the kids; he would always complain that he was tired. Now you know if you're not putting time into your marriage it makes room for the enemy. It gives Satan a foothold to begin to try to destroy what you are building.

I went to work one Monday morning. I remember it clearly because it was raining so badly and storming violently. I did not know that I was going to be walking in the storm to get to work. I walked in my supervisor's office and she started screaming and throwing things. I had been on vacation for a week. I came back, and she told me that we got audited, and in the past, we had been getting a 100%. This time we wound up getting a 97%. I told her that I thought that was good; we were only off by a little bit. I began to say to her, "Please relax," She was so upset! I asked her what was really going on because we got a good score. "Is there something you and I need to talk about?" I asked. She told me yes. She said while I was gone on vacation, four employees had been calling off work. I noticed her voice had started raising up real loudly at me. She told me that she wanted me to write them up for them not showing up to work. I asked her if we could sit down with them and talk about them making sure their attendance was good. I asked if we could give them a warning. As a mother, I knew how it was when things come up when you have small children, so I was able to understand both sides of the issue. The four employees that she was talking about would never really call off, so I couldn't put my finger on what was really going on.

Besides them calling off, there was something bigger behind all this. I stayed in her office until she became calm, and she agreed to allow me to talk to the four employees. I talked to all of them individually, and each employee stated to me that they would work on improving their attendance.

I got off work and made it home around 7:00 p.m. that evening. I got a phone call at about 8:30 p.m. from a young lady. She told me that I did not know her, but I knew her sister Michelle. I asked her how I could help her. She told me she was sorry to call me with bad news. I asked her what she was talking about and she said, "I know your son because this lady at work has pictures of your son and your husband on her desk." They had taken family pictures together. She told me that she was warning me that my husband was having an affair with this young lady at work. She went on to say to me that my husband was planning to divorce me. I said, "Wait a minute, who did you say gave you my phone number?" I told her what she was saying was foolish. I thanked her for the call, and for what she was telling me. I told her I would follow up on it, and that this phone call was very disturbing for me. I mentioned to her that I would be calling her sister Michelle, and she said that would be fine because she knew about it as well. When I got that phone call, I thought about the scripture John 10:10: "The thief comes only to steal, kill, and destroy. But I have come in order that you might have life - life in all its fullness." I could not rest from getting that call, so I called my friend Michelle. She picked up the phone and said, "Hey Alisha! I haven't talk to you in a while." I told her that her sister had called me with some disturbing news. "Your sister said that my husband is having an affair. Is this true?" She told me that it was true, and she wanted to tell me, but she didn't know how. She found out about my husband's affair through her sister. She said that my husband was going to divorce me. She told me that she was so sorry to give me that disturbing news, and I asked what kind of friend would not even mention it to me. I told her that my husband and her husband were best friends, and I thought she and I were friends as well. I told her that the phone call was disturbing for me. When I got off the phone with her I began to pray, and I said, "Lord help my marriage, and please don't let my husband divorce me. God don't let him leave me and my kids." I didn't know what I would do if this were to happen. After that, I called my best friend and asked her if she would pray with me concerning my marriage. I told her I received a phone call from a lady with some very disturbing news. I burst out crying and I asked my best friend what was I going to do? What were my kids and I going to do? She told me to not believe that phone call, and that we were going to trust God and believe God for my marriage. She prayed over me and told me to stay focused and to trust God. She said we didn't know for sure whether any of this was true or not, so we began to pray for my husband and my marriage. I said to my best friend, "I'm not prepared for this!" I said I couldn't believe it and that I didn't see this coming. My best friend stated to me that when the devil comes, he doesn't prepare us, he doesn't let us know, but God will always let us know because He has our backs. God wins on every hand and Satan loses. I was trying to stay focused and believe what we prayed about, and I was spending time with the word of God by looking up scriptures like Isaiah 41:10-13: "Fear not, for I am with you; be not dismayed, for I am your God: I will Strengthen you, Yes I will help you I will uphold you with my righteous right hand. For I, am the Lord your God."

I was trying to say focused and lean on the Word of God throughout the week. When I felt like I had too much pressure on me, from time to time I would feel my heart beat extremely fast. I would have panic attacks that felt like heart attacks. I would try to keep my mind on God, but I would burst out and start crying. I would try to keep my mind on God but every now and then, that phone call would try to haunt me. I kept speaking over my marriage. I kept pleading the blood of Jesus over my marriage.

The weekend came, and my husband came home. He was happy and in a good mood. He hung out with the kids, and took us to the movies. I made up my mind that I wasn't going to bring it up, so I didn't because I thought maybe it wasn't true. That weekend was special to me and it felt like when we first got married. We felt so in love and were enjoying one another so much. Right after the movies we took the kids to the park and my husband and I sat down to talk. I began to talk about our marriage, and I asked my husband if there was one thing I could change in our marriage to become a better wife. He began to name things that I could not even believe he was saying. He told me I needed to cook more, and I needed to look more attractive as a young lady. He said I needed to lose a little weight because I was gaining weight. He told me that I spent too much time at the church, and he told me since we got married I have changed. He told me when he first met me, we would hang out, go to the movies, go out to eat, and go to the nightclub. He told me we didn't do that anymore. We were sitting down at the time. I immediately stood up and told him to look me eye and say that he wasn't having an affair on me. When I said that, his eyes got big. He looked like he was in shock, like he couldn't believe I had found out that he had someone else. He told me that he wasn't happy anymore. I asked him if he was involved with another woman, and he told me he was.

I had to have Faith in God. Even though my husband was saying all those terrible things to me, I had to hold on to faith. That was going to help strengthen me, because I was going to need it. I had so much going on! First with my job and now with my husband, and it appeared that things were only going to get worse. I had been on vacation from work. After I get back from vacation, I received a phone call from a manager; she wanted to see me in her office. I went to her office, and she wanted to let me that know that my boss was getting ready to fire me. She told me they'd had a meeting two days prior, and my boss was going around telling people how she wanted to terminate me, and that she had another lady in mind that she wanted to hire for the position. She had spoken with Judy and asked her why she was terminating me. She tried to say it was because I was lacking in my job performance. She asked Judy if she had sat down and talked with me, or if she gave me a warning to let me know the areas that needed improvement. My supervisor indicated that she had not talked to me, and I was not working out anyway. She had told my supervisor that all the other managers did not believe what she was saying about me. I thanked her for letting me know what was going on and told her that I did not see any of this coming. I told her I noticed three weeks ago that my boss had been picking at me for every little thing, and she was constantly on my back. I thanked her again and told her that I was planning to resign that day and give my two weeks' notice. I shared with her that I was looking to go to nursing school. She told me she that would be good for me and I would be a good nurse.

Right after that, I left her office and as soon as I made it back to my office, my boss called me on the phone and told me she wanted to talk to me; she said that it was very important. I went to her office and she told me to come in. Right as I was getting ready to shut the door, the security officer came in behind me. She asked me if I had anything to say before we started the meeting. I told her, "Yes, I wanted to first thank you for the opportunity that you gave me as a supervisor, and thank you for all the experience that I received with the company." I told her I was so grateful to be a part of this company, and I also stated that I was turning in my two weeks' notice that day. "As of February 2, 1990, I will be stepping down from the position as a supervisor." She looked at me with a look of shock on her face, because she was not expecting me to step down. Her intention was to fire me at the meeting, and she thought I was going to be upset when she terminated me. That is why she had the security officer come to the meeting. I was very professional, and that day was special because it was also my birthday. I just believe thatGod had that manager to call me and let me know what was going on, so I would not be in the dark. I was so happy that I didn't get fired, and I was able to turn in my two weeks' notice. Judy told me I didn't have stay for two weeks; she said that I had two weeks of vacation and she was going to let me take my last two weeks of vacation. She also blessed me with my last bonus check, and it was $600.00. I was just smiling and praising God at the same time. I really needed that bonus check and it came right at a time when I really needed it.

I asked my supervisor what would happen to my brother as the head cook, and she assured me that my brother would be fine. He would remain the head cook, and he continued to work there for about eight years. I cleaned out my office and I started my vacation. Judy called me in the office and told me that they would mail my last check to me. I told my coworkers that they would be fine and to continue to do what they needed to do to keep their jobs. I told them that I would miss them, and some of them asked me for my phone number. I told them that I would take their numbers down, and I would keep in touch.

While I was off work, I started looking for job. I was hired by another hospital as a patient care technician, and my duties were to assist the nurses with vital signs, to bathe patients, and to assist with patient discharges. I worked 72 hours every two weeks, and that was considered full time. I found that I liked helping patients so much that I wanted to go back to school to get my nursing degree. But I would get off work and find myself just staying in my room, isolating myself and not going anywhere or wanting to be around anyone.

On my days off I wouldn't do anything but sleep. My girlfriend would come over to help me with the kids because she knew I was getting so stressed and depressed that my stomach would be in knots. My husband had checked out of the marriage mentally, and I was left to try to do everything on my own. I was starting to have some health issues; I could not even eat because whatever I would eat, I would just throw it back up. I couldn't keep anything down on my stomach. I began to hear voices. One Saturday morning and I heard a voice telling me to go take the gun and kill my husband. So, I got up and went to get the gun and I stood over my husband with the gun in my hand. The voices told me to shoot him and then take my own life because I wouldn't be worth anything anyway. Immediately I heard someone knocking very loudly at the door. My husband woke up saw me standing over him with the gun. He jumped up and ran to the door, and the person who was at the door was my best friend Janice. They began to beg and plead with me to put the gun down, to please put the gun down. I was looking at both of them like "what are you talking about?" because I did not even know that I had the gun in my hand. That's how bad the depression had gotten for me. My husband took the gun and my girlfriend grabbed me and began praying over me. She cried out in a loud voice in anger and sympathy for me and for the things I was going through, and I began to cry as well. Tears began to roll down my eyes. I cried, "I can't believe this is happening!" I was supposed to be happy with my husband and my two kids, and instead I felt all alone. I did not know I had checked out mentally. It was so bad that I was going to become a murderer, and that was not me! I was doing something that I wasn't even aware of. I'm telling you hearing voices is real! People say that you cannot hear voices, but you can. Depression is real. Suicide is real.

Whoever is reading this book: if you're going through something, please get help! Please call your local suicide hotline or call 911. Do not be alone and tell somebody what you are going through. I told my husband I was sorry for even trying to take his life. I told him that I been under so much stress due to the marriage and that if he wanted out, I would not hold him anymore. "If you want out, I will give you a divorce," I told him. It wasn't healthy for me or the kids. It wasn't healthy for them to see me going through all this anguish, and I didn't feel right being in the shape that I was in. My girlfriend stated to my husband that she would come and help me out with the kids and be here for us. She even prayed for my husband at the time. Right after that he packed his clothes and he was gone for two weeks I did not know where he was staying. The following week, I went to see a lawyer and filed for the divorce. The same week he was served with divorce papers by an officer.

My husband moved out two weeks later, but during the time he was there, he was very mean to me. I could never talk to him about anything. My mortgage was three months behind, and he had stopped paying all the bills, so everything was left on me. My mortgage was $785, my car payment was $365, and I still had utilities that needed to be paid and food to buy. There were times when my kids and I wouldn't have any food in the refrigerator. I went to the church and asked if they could help me pay my utility bills and give me a food a voucher. Looking back on it, I was still being blessed. God was still in the blessing business, and sometimes I would come home and find money in my mailbox. Another time I came home, and there were five bags of groceries on my front porch. God was still watching over me and he was sustaining me. On top of everything else, while I was going through my divorce, my mother passed away. I was dealing with death of my mother and my husband's infidelity. Losing my mom was particularly tough, because we hadn't always enjoyed a healthy relationship. My relationship with my mother had recently gotten much better, I had worked on building our relationship, and I loved my mother very much. Even though she had not raised me, my mother would take turns spending the night at her children's houses, and as we got older she would come over every other weekend and spend time with me and her grandkids. She apologized that she wasn't around when I was growing up. I told her it was okay. My mom and I were catching up on old times and I was grateful to have those great moments and times with her. I became close to her and I know my mother loved me. My grandmother would always tell me that she loved me even though she didn't raise me, but that love was confirmed as my mother and I repaired our relationship. Whoever is reading this book, I just want to say to you that if you have some problems with your mother, and maybe you haven't talked in years, please pick up the phone and call your mother. Talk to your mother, don't let another day go by without calling her. I waited until my twenties to build a relationship with my mother, but God allowed us to work things out. I was 28 years old when I started to build a relationship with her, and I was grateful to have that bond with her at that time in my life before she passed away. She was a beautiful young lady who loved the Lord and always talked about Jesus to anyone who would listen to her. I believe that my fire and zeal for the Lord came from my mother, because she loved God and I love Him too. My mother passed away on March 7, 2003. Rest in peace, Mom. I will see you again.

My divorce was finalized in 2004. I could not stay in the house because I could not afford it. I was able to sell the house and after everything was paid off, I was left with $4000. I was still going through depression, so I decided to go ahead a make an appointment to see a counselor. What I soon learned was that going to a counselor just opened me up emotionally and then shut me down too quickly. I was unable to work through a lot of what I needed to talk about since the sessions only lasted one hour. I'm telling you after leaving the counseling session I was so down, and I called my girlfriend on the phone to ask if she would pray with me. I suffered severe depression! She began to pray with me and kept telling me to trust God. She invited me to a prayer breakfast that was coming up on Saturday morning. She told me I needed to be there, and that this would really help me. She said there was another young lady that was going through a difficult time, and she would be sharing her testimony about her battles against thoughts of suicide and her battle with depression. I showed up at the prayer breakfast and the young lady discussed her life story, her battles with depression, and some suicidal thoughts that she was having. As she spoke, I couldn't stop crying. I found myself just shaking and crying and receiving her testimony. I began to speak over myself. I began to say, "Self you are healed." I started naming all of my issues one by one. I said, "In the name of Jesus I am healed." I began to call everything out that I was battling: depression, anxiety, low self-esteem, fear, isolation, and hearing voices. I knew when I started speaking on my healing that I was getting stronger and stronger.

After the prayer breakfast was over with, I went up and talked to the young lady and I thanked her so much for being open and letting God use her. I told that she didn't know how much hearing her testimony was helping me and that I was battling with depression and suicide. I told her that I was going to declare and decree for my healing to take place immediately, and that I knew I still had to align my spirit with the Word of God. While I was going through different things in my life, I would look up scriptures that talked about fear, or I would look up scriptures on faith. That's how I was able to build my faith, and that's how I was able to overcome and remove the fear and the isolation and anxiety out of my life. I believe that the invitation to that breakfast was God once again looking out for me.

I was practicing celibacy and I wasn't dating or seeing anyone. I was spending time with God. It's important to keep in mind that when you declare and decree things over your life, you are going to be tested. I just believe that trials come in triples, but come only to make you stronger. You must be careful about what you speak out of your mouth because it can come to pass. Yes, I spoke about my healing and the very thing that I said came back on me. I will say I must have been doing something right because I felt myself getting stronger. I was reading the Word of God, but I would still go through trials and tribulations and I had to lean on the scriptures.

My daughter was away at college, and she phoned me one day to say she was calling to check on me and that she was concerned about me. I was still hearing voices from time to time, but I was doing better. I started talking to her about the life insurance policy because I was just making sure she knew where everything was. She started saying, "Mom, why are you talking to me like that? You are scaring me, and you're not going anywhere. You are going to be around for a long time. God has a lot of work for you to do, Mama, and you have so many testimonies and so many people you are going to help when they hear or read your story one day. Mama, you are so strong." I wanted to change the subject, so I thanked my daughter for calling to check on me. She had started calling me every day checking on me. When she got off the phone with me, I found out that she had found my best friend phone number and she told her that she was concerned about me. She told her I had been talking strange and would she please go over to the house to check on me because she didn't want me to be alone. One hour later, there was a loud banging on my door and I did not want to open it. It turned out that my daughter was right. The voices kept coming, and the voices were telling me to turn the gas on and take my life. My girlfriend continued to bang on the door and I asked who it is and was and she said it is Janice and open the door now. I opened the door and as soon as she walked in she looked me straight in my eyes and said, "Whatever you are going through, you are getting ready to turn all this over to God". She told me I needed to tell God all that I was going through. Janice asked me if I want to be delivered from hearing voices, from depression and suicide, and all that I was going through. She said, "Alisha, God knows all about your struggles. Do you want to be set free? Do you want to be made whole?" I said yes, and she said to me, "Everything that you lost - your husband, your house, your car, and your mind - will all be returned to you." God restored me; she prophesied to me that day and didn't even know that she was doing it. She told me, "God has a husband with your name on it and he's going to give you a house with your name. God is going to restore your credit. God is building you up, and He will return everything that was stolen from you. The only thing you must do is believe everything you are asking for right now on this day." We begin to go into prayer. I fell on my knees just crying out loud. I said to Him, "God deliver me out of the pit." I prayed for deliverance for everything that I was going through. I could feel it coming up out of my belly. I was throwing up - it was big and thick mucus. I felt all that coming up out of my belly. That's how I was able to be delivered from suicide, and from hearing voices. That day God came into my living room and healed me from all my sickness. Today I can truly say that I am healed, and I am now able to help others with depression and suicide. I know the reason why I had to go through some of the battles was, so I would be able to help somebody else one day. I give it all to God I cannot take the glory. I give the highest praise to Jesus Christ.

During this time of my life, God's grace was evident in so many ways. Even when I couldn't see it, feel it or recognize it, it was always present. Even when I look back at the times when I was struggling the most, I can see God's hand, keeping me, and I can see the favor he enacted in my life.

For example, I thank God that they had prayer in school when my daughter and I were coming up because they don't have that in our schools today. I pray for teachers that take care of children now, because they are not learning anything in our schools about God; they can't even pray in the schools anymore. Children today have to go to a Christian school to be able to pray during school. I said all that to say, as a single mother and the things I went through, God hands were still on my daughter and me.

I used to think that living with anxiety, fear and hopelessness were going to be a way of life for me. This is just the way I thought things would be, but when I came to know the Lord, and started living God's way, I began to see that all things are possible to anyone who believes and obeys God's Word. It's even possible to live without anxiety, negative fear, and hopelessness, and emotions which only God can relieve us of. We must believe when we pray. Have you ever felt as though God has forsaken you? Well, if you have, I would say you're not alone. In fact, you are in very good hands with your Father. Not only do thousands of people feel that way right now, I have felt like that from time to time, but would that make me stop believing the Word of God? Even Jesus felt that way at one time; at his lowest point in His life, Jesus said, "My God, my God why have you forsake me?"(Matthew 27:46). We all are going to have difficult times. There will be times when we all will feel alone, like when I was in abusive relationship with my ex-husband. I began to question and say where is God, and how could He let this happen to me? But I realized that He was with me. If He wasn't with me, that man probably would have killed me.

During the time, I was in the abusive relationship with my ex-husband, he began to do drugs. I will say that even though I was being abused, I knew God was taking my punches because He did that all on the cross for me. Sometimes we feel all alone and abandoned, but the truth is we aren't alone, and God is always with us to help us when we call on Him even during these times. We don't have to be controlled by our fear, anxiety, or hopelessness anymore. We can keep praying and knowing the truth of what God's word says about those things. No matter what problems we have in our lives, Jesus has overcome them all for us. We may have tribulations; but be of good cheer, Jesus has overcome the world (John 16:33).

How to Overcome Fear

- By putting all your trust in God, and turning it completely over to Jesus.

- Remember that fear is having faith in the devil and not in God.

- Remember to fear not; the shepherd is with you to train you to find comfort in Him.

- Remember to cast all your cares upon Him, for He cares for you.

Listed below are the scriptures that I lean on every day to help me remember that God is always working in my life. Take some time to study them yourself, they have the power to change your life.

Hebrews 11:1-6
Romans 10: 9
Mark 11:22-24
Hebrews 4:16
1 Timothy 6:12
John 3:27

Always remember that His grace is sufficient! Grace can be defined as God's unmerited favor over the lives of His children. When we are in the midst of our troubles, favor can be difficult to identify. It can seem as though God has forsaken us. But we cannot afford to forget that God said He would never leave us or forsake us! Favor is still favor, even when we are unable to identify it! God favored me when he blessed me with a supervisory position at the hospital. He favored me when He made it possible for me to purchase my first home. He favored me when he protected me during an abusive marriage. He favored me when He had the manager call to warn me about my supervisor's plan to terminate me. He favored me when He sent my friend Janice to my door to pray for me in my darkest moment, when I was close to taking my own life. God's grace never fails! It is up to us to recognize it for what it is.

The suffering that I endured only perfected God's

strength, and it prepared me for the next stage in my journey toward learning how to heal. Now that I was delivered and my faith restored, it was time to get stronger, and for God to show Himself mighty in new ways in my life – ways that I had not seen before.

Reflections

Questions

1. We all experience fear from time to time. What is your greatest fear? How have you maintained power over it?

2. Define grace. Recount instances during your life when you knew God's grace was presence?

3. How do have remain encouraged during difficult seasons of your life?

Reflections

Reflections

Reflections

Reflections

3 GROWTH

By God's power, I had been delivered of my sadness, my fear, my anxiety, and my depression. He sent help and encouragement in my lowest moments. He provided reminders when it was hard for me to see my own way out. He restored my mind and my sanity from a low place, and now it was time to build me up. Now it was time to grow both my faith and my capacity for joy.

I left my job as a supervisor at the rehabilitation hospital in Missouri. When I initially got that position, I had to complete an eight-week class to be certified, and at the end of course, I had to take an exam. I passed with an 85% on my test and I received my certificate eight weeks later. I was able to operate as a full-time supervisor, and I held that position for six years.

When I resigned that position, I started working at a new hospital called Barnes Jewish Hospital. Before I went to nursing school, I was working as a Patient Care Tech, which is another name for nurse's assistant or CNA. Barnes Jewish Hospital offered a certification program for the CNA's, and I got my certification for the program six week later. Then I had to take an exam, and I passed. I received my certificate to work as a Patient Care Tech, and I remained in that position for about four years. Then I decided to further my education and sign up for the nursing program. I started at St. Louis Community College in 1993 in the LPN Nursing Program. I graduated from nursing school 1995. I will never forget the years when I was in nursing school, because it was hard. The classes were challenging, and I still had to work and take care of my family. Today I can truly say I love being a nurse, I love taking care of the patients. Nursing school paid off, and after graduating I was able to apply for nursing positions while I was still working. I applied online for another position at a Dialysis Center. After I applied online, a week later I got a call for an interview. I went to the interview, and a week after that I got a call back and was informed I had been selected to fill the position. God was surely growing and increasing me.

I took the position, but I had to be certified again, which would mean I would have to go through a four-week training course. The training consisted of learning how to operate the dialysis machine, how to set up the machine, and how to break down the machine. I had to make sure I knew all about Dialysis, Hemodialysis Dialysis, Peritoneal Dialysis, and all about the kidney before I was able to come out on the floor to take care of the patients. I finished my training with an "A" and I passed my exam with a 92%. I was certified as a Dialysis Nurse. At that time, I was working both jobs. I started working part time at the hospital and working full time at the Dialysis Center to catch up on my bills for the household. A year later I was able to turn in my two weeks' notice at the hospital. I continued work full time at the Dialysis Center. It became too much for me, working two jobs and I was still trying to maintain my home and family. The things that I needed to do at home, like taking care of my kids was getting harder while working two jobs. When I got off work, it would be so late that I would not have time to spend with my daughter and son, so I gave up one of the positions. I just wanted to focus on one job.

I really liked taking care of the patients at the dialysis center but the work there was fast-paced. I would have to put on three patients in the morning between 5:30 and 6:30 a.m. They would be on the machine for about three to four hours every time they came for the treatment. After those three patients finished their dialysis, I would put on three more patients because we were required to put on six patients per day. I would have to break the machine down and set it back up for the next three patients to be put on. Once the machines were finished, they had to be cleaned. I was required to assess the patients before they got on the machine. I would listen to their lungs, I would have them breathe in and out, and I would listen to their hearts. If everything looked and sounded good,

I would then hook them up to machine and set the timer for Dialysis for three to four hours. While they were on the machine, their blood was being filtered; the machine was cleaning their blood and taking all the poison out of their bodies. It was so important to watch them closely because sometimes patients will pass out while on the machine if their blood pressure is low. That's why it was so important to talk with the patient to tell them it's not good to drink too much alcohol because it made it difficult to pull all the fluid off them. The doctor would write the order based on their weight and that would determine how much we should pull off.

Working at the Dialysis Center was often challenging because we didn't know if the patient would pass out on us. The patients would be very sick. Keep in mind that their kidneys were not working properly so they are depending on the machine to clean and filter their body, taking out all the poison and toxins. I'm telling you, it would bring tears to my eyes every time I would think about the patients and what they were going through being on Dialysis. I would say to God, "Lord, I pray that You would bless all the patients with a kidney." I know that He is God; He can do anything that He wants to do, and He has the healing power. He can heal any disease, illness, or sickness because He said that we were healed by his stripes. I wanted so badly to bless somebody with a kidney. I'm telling you God heard me pray, and two years later he put it on my heart to bless a patient who was sick from all the poison that was in his body. It was God who put it in my heart to bless him with a kidney. I did not know that by speaking that prayer out loud, that two years later, I would be able to bless someone with one of my kidneys. I know Jesus can take blood and make it whole, cleaning and filteringit. We should thank God every day that we have all the use of our organs and limbs. I know sometimes I find myself taking so much for granted, but as I was working at the Dialysis center and taking care of patients, it reminded me of how blessed I was. These patients had kidneys that did not function, and I did. I will always give God all the praise for allowing me to take care of patients whose kidneys were not working. It really humbled me and made me look around and realize how blessed I am. No matter what I was going through with the battle of my divorce, being a single mother, or with my mom passing away, I was blessed. I was falling in love with Jesus and I was truly blessed to be able have all my limbs and not have to be hooked up to a machine three times a week. God promoted me to a place that made me realize I needed to stop complaining about what I was going through, because other people were going through much worse.

I want to take a break to speak to someone's heart that may be reading this book. God put it on my heart to go out and do the research and get the information on how to be a donor. I made a phone call one Monday when I was off work, at Barnes Jewish hospital. The operator connected me to a social worker who was able tell me about the requirements to become a kidney donor. I spoke with the social worker she told me the first step is the paperwork. She told me that she was sending out a package for me to fill out that included the documents I would need to complete. I was to complete the paperwork and mail it back in. She told me that once she got it back, they would look it over and give me a call, and the next step would be to come in to do blood work. Before I got ready to hang up the phone, the social worker asked me why I wanted to do this. I told her it was put on me by God to bless somebody with a kidney; I told her that I have been a Dialysis nurse for over six years. She thanked me for considering being a donor and said that she hoped it worked out. I told her that it would because God was all in it, and He was going to work it all out - someone would be blessed with my kidney. After getting off the phone with her, I got a funny feeling in my stomach; a feeling of joy arose in me. I said to God, "Whoever you want me to bless with my kidney, please show me the patient."

I was off for a week on vacation, when I received a phone call from the social worker. She told me, "I have good news: your paperwork looks good, and the next step is to make some appointments to come in and do blood work." Now keep in mind, I didn't even know who was getting the kidney. I told a social worker that was good news. I told her I was on vacation and I could do a lot of my testing while I was on vacation. She scheduled me for the next day for blood work, all my tests, and my X-rays.

Awhile later, I was at work and I went out into the waiting room to get my patient. He came back, and I weighed him. I told him that I would be putting him on today, and that I was going to be taking care of him. He told me he was so

excited for me to be his nurse today because I was a good stick. He said that when I put him on the machine his arm didn't hurt, and that I was a very caring nurse. The patient was so happy that day, and when he came in I overheard him talking to another patient and he told him he was a believer. He said he believed that he was going to get a kidney and that he was on the donors list already. He was walking by every patient's chair saying, "God told me He is going to bless me with a kidney." I'm telling you that day he was so excited, and I had never seen him so excited. You got to know a lot of the patients well because you saw them and cared for them on a regular basis. There were times when he would come in and he would be quiet, but that day he was so confident that he was going to get a new kidney. I was believing with him. While I was hooking him up to the machine, he looked me in my eyes and I could just see that his eyes were so glossy and clear. He said, "God is going to do this for me; I'm going to get a kidney." I said, "I believe with you, and it won't be too much longer. If you believe for that kidney, He will do it for you." I told him that his faith must be so strong, and he must not let anyone stand in the way of the promise that God had for him. I told him everything will line up for him because he was believing that he was going to get a new kidney. He was just like the lady with the issue of blood: she was believing for her healing; she was believing that her bleeding would dry up, and because she was believing in her healing, she was determined to be healed. She pushed her way through the crowd and
touched His cloak, and her bleeding stopped at once; and she

had the feeling inside and immediately she was healed of her trouble. So, while my patient was talking, I was believing with him.

This all happened on a Tuesday morning, and on Wednesday he was back at the Dialysis Center. This time he was so sick, and he had a lot of fluid on him. I was not taking care of him that day, but I walked over to check on him, and I told him that I was going to be praying for him. I told him to keep faith about his healing. I bent down closer to his ear and said, "Keep believing for your kidney because that's was going to give you your strength - not looking at your situation but believing in God. God is already healing you, and you have a new kidney with your name on it." The nurse was setting up the machine to try to pull off most of the fluid. As I walked away, I heard the spirit of God like He was right in my ear telling me he was the one that I was going to bless with my kidney. A tear fell from my eyes, and I began to talk to God in the spirit. I asked Him, "Are you sure he's the one?" He told me yes, and that I was not able to speak to him about it. He also shared with me that I was not to speak to my family about it. I could hardly work that day. I was sad and happy at the same time. Have you ever felt something in your belly? Have you ever been so happy on one hand, but the other hand you were nervous?

A couple of weeks went by and I got called in for a job interview at the local Veteran's Administration hospital. I went in for the interview and the supervisor told me that I would be working in extended care if I got the job. She also told me the position was an evening job, and this was a consideration because I had been working mornings. My schedule at the dialysis center called for me to work 10 hours a day; I would work four days on and three days off. She told me the new position was 3:30 p.m. to midnight. I turned down the position and told her I could not work evenings because I have a son at home that I must care for. A month later, they called me back to give me a new position in the daytime. She advised me to take the position, and once I got my foot in the door, they could work with me about my schedule. I believe this was God's doing: I turned down the position and they called me back with a new position more fitting, so I did take it. I was still working at the dialysis center, but in July of 2009 I put in my two-week notice. My supervisor told me that she was going to really miss me; all the patients were hugging me, and they were crying. They asked me to come back and visit with them, and I promised them I would keep them in my prayers and visit. At that time, I was still working on getting the information package for becoming a donor.

Before I left the dialysis, center I was able to see my patient. I will never forget it: it was on a Saturday morning, I told the patient that God was going to bless him, and I would be his kidney donor. I would be giving him my kidney. I told him he would be receiving a call to do the testing to see if we were a match. He looked at me and he began to cry. He began thanking me. I told him that it was all God; I couldn't take the credit because it all goes to God. I told him, "God showed me that you will be preaching one day; you and your wife will have your own church." He looked at me and said that he believed that also. I told him that I would not be working there anymore because I had accepted a new position at the Veteran's hospital and that today was my last day. He was also a veteran, and he was very happy for me. He told me that God was doing great things with me. He kept saying thanks, and I told him to please not mention it to anybody in the center. He said that he wouldn't, but he said that he was getting ready to call his wife and tell her the good news. I said that would be fine. He was so happy, and I was happy for him. He never gave up, and he kept believing that one day he would be healed. That there was a kidney with his name on it, and he would not have to take dialysis treatment anymore. In October I got a phone call from the social worker, and she told me the blood tests had come back, that everything was fine, and they were

ready to go to the next step. The next step was for me to come into the office to go over the procedure. I would sit down with a doctor to discuss how they would remove the kidney. She then told me we were a 100% match. I started praising God over phone and just kept saying, "God I know you are all in this."

I began working at the VA hospital on August 9, 2009 as a full-time nurse. I did not get the day shift I wanted; I was working one eight-hour day and four evening shifts, but it worked out because my best friend kept my son until I got off work. I would go into work at 3:30 in the afternoon and would get off at midnight. I worked that shift for about a year and a half. I was just starting my new job, so I had no vacation and I was still on my 90-day probation. I found myself getting nervous. and I began to pray and say "God, how are you going to do this? I do not have any time off; how am I going to pay my bills? How am I going to do this surgery?" The social worker had explained to me that I didn't have to worry about any bills for the surgery because the recipient's insurance would pay for the surgery. While I was on the phone talking with the social worker, she asked me what day I wanted to have the surgery. I told her God put it on my heart to have the surgery on November 24, 2009. Two weeks later, I was in the office of the social worker and she went over all the paperwork with me. She also asked me whether I had been offered any money for my kidney. I told her I was not offered any money. They also wanted to make sure that I was not being pressured to give up my kidney. Right after I talked with the social worker, I sat down with the doctor and he went over all my tests with me. The doctor asked me why I wanted to donate my kidney. I told him I was led by God to bless one of the patients with my kidney. He laughed real loud and looked at me strangely. He told me the day that I picked wouldn't be a good day for him to do the surgery because he was going out of town for the Thanksgiving holiday. I looked the doctor in his face and said that we must do the surgery on the date God gave me. He began to laugh out loud, and he told me they were going to reschedule the surgery. I looked at the doctor and said, "You're not the one that's going to be doing the surgery." He just kept laughing at me like everything was so funny. I was just real quiet after that and left the office and went home. The social worker called and asked me how did everything go? I told her the doctor was very rude and that he was laughing at me. She apologized for the things I was going through. I told her that I was getting discouraged and that maybe God was not telling me to do this. She told me no, we were going to continue to go on with the plans and the doctor who would do the kidney surgery would be calling me. God gave me the number one doctor to do my surgery on November 24th. When I talked to the doctor, he explained to me how he would remove my kidney. He said that due to some previous surgeries I'd had, he would not be able to go through my stomach. He said sometimes Black Americans have a lot of scar tissue from previous surgeries. The doctor explained he would go in through my left side to remove my kidney, and he would have to cut through my rib cage. He assured me that everything would be fine and said the surgery would take about six or seven hours. He asked me if I had any questions. I asked him how long I would need to be off work, and he told me it would take about six to eight weeks before I would be able to return to work. I thanked the doctor for all the information. He was so nice, and he answered all my questions. Before we get off phone he told me I was in good hands and the surgery was going to be fine.

On Monday morning I went into work at the VA hospital. I went straight in to my supervisor's office; I told her I needed to talk with her and that it was very important. She thanked me for coming and said she wanted to go over my 90-

day performance review anyway. I stated to her that I was a kidney donor and that I was going to be donating my kidney to save someone's life. I told her my surgery would be on November 24th. I told her I would have to be off work for about six to eight weeks to recover from the surgery. I told her I knew I didn't have any accumulated time off because I hadn't even completed my 90-day probationary period. She smiled at me and told me that was fine, and they would allow me time off to have the surgery. She also stated that I would need to write a letter and that she would write one also on my behalf to her supervisor. She then told me they had a kidney donor program at the Veteran's hospital, and if I got approved I would not lose any time and I would get paid while I was off work. I would still be able to accumulate vacation and holiday pay while I was off. I must give God all the praise and all the glory. I said, "look at God!" I knew this is all God because who gets paid for being off work when they haven't even been on the job for 90 days.

My supervisor went over my 90-day performance review. She told me I had a good performance review and I received a rate of outstanding in every category. She stated that my attendance was perfect, and all the staff loved me. I thanked my supervisor for allowing me to go out to have the surgery. She told me she understood because members of her family struggled with kidney failure. Two weeks later, my supervisor told me that I had been approved for the kidney program and I was so happy. I kept saying I know this is God. I called the social worker on Monday and told her my job had given me approval to be off, and she could go ahead and schedule the surgery for November 24th.

The surgery was scheduled, and I had to be there at 5:30 a.m. The recipient's family was there, and the surgery went well. We were only in surgery for two hours and the patient that received the kidney was doing well. After the surgery, my convalescence went well and the patient was also recovering well. We both went home four days later. The patient's sister-in-law asked if she could take care of me after I went home for the week. She said she would like to take care of me and make sure I was okay, and I agreed to allow her to care for me. I thank God for my family, my Church family, and my friends at the Veteran's hospital who were very supportive. When I got to the hospital the day of the surgery, one of my close sisters in Christ, Imani, met me there and prayed over me and the family. Imani stayed with me until the surgery was over, and I will never forget how she was there for me during that time. I love her dearly and she is like my special sister. I can report that the family that received my kidney is doing well. It has been nine years since the transplant. He is doing well, and he is now a full-time Pastor and his lovely wife is an Evangelist. They had three children, two daughters and one son. His two daughters are in the ministry. One of his daughters is a youth minister and his son is also a minister. I'm telling you God is good! He took a part of me and used it to expand and increase an entire family and an entire ministry! Talk about growth!

I remember this day like it was yesterday: it was a Friday morning, July 23, 2010. My coworker asked me whether I knew a man name Howard Tyrone Thorpe. I told her no and asked why she was asking. She told me she just wanted to know if I knew him. When I looked at his name on the board it said that he was a shop steward and he was a member of the union. He was also the Chaplain for the Union. My coworker came to my department around 12:00 noon and asked me if I would go with her down into the basement. I thought we were going down to the basement for me to pray with her because we had done this previously. I didn't know that she was taking me down to the basement for me to meet Howard Tyrone Thorpe. As soon the elevator door opened, I saw a young man wearing a blue shirt and white pants. He had a big smile on his face. My co-worker said, "Alisha meet Tyrone and Tyrone meet Alisha." Right after she introduced us, she got back on the elevator and left the two of us standing there looking at each other. Tyrone told me that he worked in the kitchen as a supervisor and a cook. I told him that I had seen him around the hospital. He gave me his card with his name on it and it said Minister Tyrone Thorpe. He began to tell me a little about himself, and he told me that he had been working for the veteran's hospital for over 34 years. He also served in the United States Army for four years and spent three years in the Army Reserves. He also told me he had been single for seven years. I told him that I was not looking for a relationship and he told me he was not trying to pick me up. He said he was just telling me a little bit about himself. I thanked him for sharing that with me but stated once again that I was not looking to be in relationship right then. I thanked him for his card and got back on the elevator.

The same day I went to my coworker I asked her what she was trying to do, and she told me she wanted me to meet him because he was a Godly man and he was a minister at his church. She told me he was single, and he was praying for a wife. I thanked my coworker for thinking about me, but I was not interested in dating. Weeks went by and it would seem like I would see him every other day. I remember one day seeing him ride a ten-speed bike, and another time I saw him riding a go cart. One day Tyrone stopped to ask me if I needed a ride back to my department and I told him no, but I asked him if he would take my coworker back to her department. I said she was on medication and she was pregnant. Tyrone looked at me with a big smile on his face, and I 'm telling you, I have never seen a man smile like him. He would just show all his teeth, and every time I saw him he was always happy.

Three weeks later, I was sitting in my car and I decided to call my best friend Janice whom I hadn't seen in about two weeks because I'd moved back to Saint Louis, MO. I had found a home there and I was going to rent to own. I called Janice to ask her if she wanted to go see the movie *For Colored Girls*. The date was August 5, 2010. She asked what time the movie started, and I told her I would call her back and let her know what time it began. I hung up the phone and ordered the tickets for the movie. As I put my debit card back in my purse, the business card Minister Tyrone gave me fell out of my wallet. I said this prayer, "God if it is meant for me to call him, give me a sign." God showed me his big beautiful smile as a sign. I dialed his number and he answered the phone on the second ring. "May I speak to Minister Tyrone?" and he responded, "Praise the Lord."

He sounded like he was very happy to receive my phone call. He said he thought I was never going to call him, and that he was so grateful that I had called. He asked me how my day was going, and whether I had any plans for that Friday. I told him yes, my girlfriend and I were going to see a movie. He asked me what movie we were going to see, and I told him that I bought two tickets to go see the movie *For Colored Girls*. He then asked me what time the movie started, and I told him that he couldn't go with us to the movies because my girlfriend and I were hanging out. He told me that he was not trying to go with us, he just wanted to know what time the movie started because he wanted to go see the movie also. I told him it was nice talking to him and I would call him back a little later. Tyrone said that would be fine and he would be looking forward to my phone call. I got off the phone with Minister Tyrone and I called my girlfriend back and told her the movie started at 7:00 p.m. She told me sorry, but she was not able to go at that time. So, I called Minister Tyrone back and asked him if he would still like to go to the movie with me since my best friend was unable to go. He said, "Yes!" real loud into the phone. He had a deep voice and when he spoke, his voice carried. I told him that I had not eaten, and that I was going to Applebee's to eat something before the movie started. He asked if he could join me for dinner so that we would have a chance to talk and get to know one another. He stated that he didn't want to push himself on me, but I told him that was fine, and I would see him at Applebee's.

I was at the restaurant for about 20 minutes when a young man came in the door, dressed in a nice suit. I look up and it was Minister Tyrone walking towards me. When I saw him, my heart began to beat so fast, because he looked totally different from how he looked at work in his uniform. I said to myself, "Lord he is so handsome I could just kiss him," but that was just a thought that came in my mind. You must remember that I had been celibate for eight years. We both greeted each other, and Minister Tyrone thanked me for sitting down with him so he could get to know me. He thanked me for allowing him to go to the movies with him, and then he mentioned that he had been praying for a wife and that he was not looking for a girlfriend. He was a not looking for a one-night stand or for someone to just go to bed with. He also told me that he was saving himself for his wife and that he had been practicing celibacy for seven years. I did not say anything; I was quiet and listening, but under my breath I was saying to myself, "I'm not that type of woman". Immediately and almost without thinking I just spoke out loud what I had been saying to myself. I said to him, "I'm not that type of woman. I have been practicing celibacy for eight years, and I am not that type of woman." I let him know that I was serious about practicing celibacy. I let him know that I had turned everything over to God and that included my body. I told him that I was not even dating anyone because I wanted to be serious in my relationship with God. I told him that God was the center of my life and that my desire was to be married and to be happy. When he was talking to me, I just began to speak in the spirit to God. I kept praying, "Whoever comes into my circle God, they must be sent by You and only You." I was saying to God, "I can't have any more setbacks. If he isn't the one you have sent me, end it right now."

Minister Tyrone began to tell me about himself and the struggles that he went through. He told me that he was once hooked on drug, but now he was hooked on Jesus. He said that he used to be an alcoholic, that he had cirrhosis of the liver, and that he used to have Hepatitis C. I looked at him and said, "Wow you had all that going, but God." Minister Tyrone shared with me how he overcame all battles that he had gone through and how God delivered him from crack and cocaine. He told me that while he was in the crack house he would pray to God and tell Him that if He didn't hear his cry, he was going to die from this habit. He would talk to God and say, "If you are God, deliver me from this crack." He told God he didn't want to be delivered for four to five months and then go back; he wanted to be delivered forever. He told me God healed him while he was in the crack house. He believed in his healing and because he believed, he was healed.

While he was telling me his story, I couldn't hold back my tears, I was just crying and thanking God for his healing. Sometimes while he was talking, his voice would carry and the people in the restaurant would look over at us, but that day I did not care who heard him because he was so excited. The waitress kept coming by asking if we needed anything, but it was like she was eavesdropping. She told him that she heard his testimony and she was praising God for his deliverance. When he finished giving me his testimony, I asked him how long it took for him to be clean from doing drugs and drinking, and he said that it happened that day. I want to encourage anybody that is reading this book today to know, that if He did it for Tyrone, He will do it for you, if you believe. He also told me that he had been married twice and that the first time he got married, he was 19 years old. He said he had a daughter during his first marriage and had been married for ten years. His second marriage lasted for four years and didn't work out because she started using drugs. He tried to help her get off drugs, but she would leave the house and stay out all night and sometimes be gone for a week. I could not eat my food because I was listening to him as he was telling me about his entire life. He told me that he was a changed man and God has been using him mightily. He said he prayed to God that he would be forgiven for the two failed marriages. He said that during his first marriage he was young, and he didn't know what true love was, but his first wife wanted the marriage to work. However, he was so grateful to have a daughter out of that marriage. He talked about his daughter to me all that day - how beautiful she was and the things that she was doing in life and how he was so proud of her with the degrees that she had earned. But one of the things he said he told her was that she could get all the degrees she wanted, but he wanted her to fall in love with Jesus.

Minister Tyrone told me that was his story and I told him that we had a lot in common. I began to share with him that I had been married twice also. I told him that in my first marriage I was physically and verbally abused, and in my second marriage there was a lot of mental abuse. I shared with him how when I was in the mentally abusive relationship, I battled with hearing voices and how God had healed me on my living room floor from all the things that I was going through. I told him I did believe his testimonies and that miracles happen every day; he was looking at a miracle. We sat there looking at each other and thought about the things that I had gone through and he went through. We both said at the same time, "God is good."

I shared with him that I was a kidney donor and that I only had my right kidney. I told him how God had put it on my heart to donate my kidney. I told him about the patient I had at the dialysis center that I used to take care of, and how I was a 100% match to donate my kidney to him. He said he was praying for love and that he was looking at the gift of love. We both had used so much tissue because we were crying at each other's testimony. I was so interested in sharing our testimonies that I didn't get a chance to eat my food, so I asked the waitress to box it up for me. It was getting late and was time for us to go to the movies. As we were walking into the movies, he tried to pay me for the movie. I told him the movie was already paid for, and I thanked him for the dinner. After the movie was over, he walked me back to my car. He toldme he enjoyed the date and that he prayed that we would be able to see each other again. I thanked him, and I told him I had a good time as well. When I got in my car, I kept praising God for meeting Minister Tyrone, a good Christian man. He called me that night to see if I made it home and I told him I did. We talked for about five hours on the phone, just talking about God and life.

I felt so happy every time we talked on the phone, and I would just light up like a Christmas tree whenever I saw him or talked to him on the phone. Tyrone was working days at the Veteran's hospital and I was working evenings, so when he could he would call me during his lunch break or he would call me on his way to work. I didn't have to be at work until 3:30 p.m., and I didn't get off until midnight and he would get off at 3:30 p.m., so we were working opposite schedules. We were trying to set up a time to go on another date and I told Tyrone I would need to look at my work schedule. We finally came up with a day and time for a second date, and I met Tyrone at a restaurant called Lottawatta Creek.

Tyrone and I would be on the phone and we would talk about God a lot. He would pray every morning when we he called, and every night before we got off the phone. I'm telling you he was a praying man. Tyrone and I found we had a lot in common, and we really enjoyed our conversations. I felt good when I was talking with him. When I got to the restaurant where we were meeting for our second date, Tyrone was already there. When I walked in, and as I was walking towards him, he just began to smile so big. He had such an amazing smile, and all you could see were his teeth. He seemed so happy to see me. He got up and greeted me and took my coat and hung it up; he was such a gentleman. After I sat down, he said, "Tell me all about your day and how your day went." In addition to being a nurse, I am also a hairdresser and I graduated from cosmetology school in 2005. I love doing hair as a hobby of mine. I must give thanks to God because he truly blessed my hands; I can do anything with my hands because they are blessed. I can make and design things, and I am very creative. When Tyrone asked me about my day, I told him that it was very long and that I was very tired because I worked overtime on Friday, and that Saturday morning I had five clients. I explained that was why I was a little late getting to the restaurant. He said I see you have been busy and then he asked me why I was working so much. I told him that I was divorced, and I had to work extra hours to try and have enough money to support my son and daughter. I told him that my daughter was in college and I had to help her with tuition, and still have enough to pay my bills. I told him I just got a new car and I had to pay the taxes on my car. I needed the money and that's why I had been working so much overtime and doing extra hair appointments.

The waitress came over and we stopped talking to

place our order. Every time I came to this restaurant, I always ordered the catfish platter that includes three sides. Tyrone always ordered soul food. While we were waiting for our food, Tyrone opened this magazine that he had with him. He opened it to a page with wedding rings on it and asked me, "When you get married again which ring would you like?" I told him, "Wow you speak like I'm getting ready to be married," and he told me yes. He said, "You told me that your desire was to be married, that God was going to send you a husband, and that He was going to drop him down from heaven." I said, "Yes, that is my desire and yes, I am praying that God will bless me with my husband." I looked in the magazine; there were so many rings to pick from, and they were very expensive. I looked at this one ring. It looked like it was made for a princess, with the cut diamonds. I pointed to the $400 ring. Tyrone asked, "Are you sure that is the ring? Because it is cheap!" I said, "Yes, I have learned that it is not about how much you spend on the ring that make the marriage, but it is the love that the two of you have for one another. It not the size of the diamond, it is about how you show love." I looked him in the eye and said to him, "When God sends me my husband, I'm going to put all my love into the marriage and not in the diamond." I told him that in the past I looked at material things, but I told him how God had healed me from that as well. He made me see it, because I had gone from a lot of material things to having nothing. I was able to look at life totally different. I could now truly appreciate what I had. I said to Tyrone, "Don't get me wrong, there is nothing wrong with having a beautiful ring, but that's not what is most important. The ring plays a part, and it's a symbol when you are exchanging your wedding vows unto God. I don't want my marriage to be about the ring or the diamonds. I want my marriage to be about God and true love." He said that he had never heard a woman talk like that.

I said after what I had gone through in my last marriage, I had been praying this time for a godly husband. For a man who feared God, a man who had respect for God, a man who put God first and then his wife. I was praying for a saved man; I was praying for a man who would study together with me and read the Bible together with me. I told Tyrone that I wanted my husband to be the head of my household and the Pastor and the Priest of my house and be someone who would not be afraid to teach the Bible to me as I was still eager to learn all that God had for me. I'm telling you we were having some deep conversations. Tyrone went on to say, "I have been praying for wife like you." He said he had asked God to bless him with a saved wife, someone that didn't want to just go to bed with him. Tyrone said that he was going to marry me. I looked at him and smiled, but in the back of my mind I kept saying, "I heard that before." I told Tyrone that deep down in my heart my desire was to be married to a godly husband. I know I was doing everything right this time; I was not going out on dates and I was not going to be sleeping around. I was saving myself for my special husband. God was going to drop him down from heaven. I praying that I would receive that blessing from God. We finished dinner and Tyrone walked me to my car and opened the car door for me. I called him when I got home, and we talked on the phone for about four to five hours. We talked about marriage and we talked about God. It was well past midnight when we got off the phone. The next morning Tyrone called me, and he was so excited. He told me that he was praying to God about how to help me with the sales tax for my car. He said please just listen and just hear him. He said he would like to bless me with the money to pay my sales tax, which was $850. I told him I appreciated the offer, but he didn't have to do that. He said that he wanted to and that he would give me a check for that amount the next time we were together.

The following week I invited him over to my house, I told him I wanted to cook for him for Thanksgiving, and I thought it was time for him to meet my son. I worked until midnight, and when I got off, I started cooking I didn't go to bed until 4:00 a.m. that morning. Tyrone came the next day. He met my son, and then we sat down to eat Thanksgiving dinner. He told me that I didn’t have to cook all this food but that it was delicious. He said that my greens tasted better than his and that he loved the dressing; he said it was so good I could sell it in the store. We had an early Thanksgiving dinner because I was scheduled to work that night. My son really liked him; they seemed to get along well, and their conversation was good.

We would talk on the phone as much as we could, and we finally made plans to go out on a third date. We went to the movies that night and early the next day he had planned a trip to take me to Saint Louis to The Butterfly House. It was so romantic! I had never visited there; it showed you how the butterflies were created from a caterpillar to a butterfly. We were inside the butterfly house and it was amazing! The butterflies were so beautiful. They were landing all over us; they were on my head and shoulders, and I was even able to hold one in my hand. The day was so hot, but I didn't care because I loved butterflies. Tyrone told me he wanted to bring me there because I was so beautiful, just like the butterfly. I told him that I really liked being here with him that day and that it was so romantic. After we left the butterfly house, we went to a movie and then he dropped me back off at my home. Tyrone was truly a gentleman all the times we were out together. When we were out on a date, we never held hands or kissed. When he dropped me off at home, he would shake my hand. That was strange, but I knew he wanted to respect me and he truly was a gentleman. We would never go over to each other's house late at night.

As the relationship started to get serious, we talked about the churches that we were attending. I was a member of a Baptist church; the name of the church was Zion Travels Baptist church, and I had been there for five years. He told me that he was a minister and he was also a Sunday School teacher. He said he could not miss his church. But he told me that he would talk to the pastor and see if he could visit my church one Sunday. With his pastor's approval, he chose a Sunday in December, and we decided he would pick me up. When he came to pick me up, it was snowing, and he was in an accident.

His truck spun off the road and hit a wall. By the time he got to my house, he had a bruise on the top of his head, so I got him some ice to put on his face. I asked him if he wanted to go to the hospital and he said no, because we were on our way to church. That morning we were going to Sunday School at my church. It started at 8:30 a.m. but we didn't get there until 9:00 a.m. You know how it is when you haven't dated in a while and all of a sudden you bring somebody to the church. Everybody wanted to know who he was, including my pastor!

On Sunday, December 3, 2010 my son and I went over to Minister Tyrone house to go to church with him. He called me on the phone and told me to come about 8:00 a.m. because he wanted to take my son Malcolm and me out for breakfast before we went to church. When we got to his house, he invited us in. Once we were inside, he fell on his knees. He looked at Malcolm and said, "Malcolm, I want to ask you if I can marry you mom. I will love her, I will cherish her, I will take care of you and your mom, and I want to love both of you. Do I have your blessing to propose to your mother?" My son Malcolm said, "Yes, I see that you are making her happy. I see that she is smiling. I see that you are giving her flowers, teddy bears, and cards." Tyrone got up from off his knees in front of Malcolm and he fell on his knees right in front of me. He says to me, "My love will you marry me? I have been praying for the gift of love, and I'm looking at the gift of love." He said that through all the things that he went through, he never gave up on true love. He said, "I didn't look at you to undress you. What I saw when I looked at you was the gift of love." I told him yes, yes, I will marry him! He told me this one day is like a thousand years unto the Lord. He told me though we didn't know each other well, the most important thing was that he knew I loved God and he loved God.

Right after Tyrone proposed to me, I jumped up and start praising God. I said, "Honey I have been praying for a husband and I did not give up!" I told him when I was seven years old, God told me everything that was spoken over me. God said to me, "You will be married; you will have a husband that would love you unconditionally." He told me I would be able to be a good Christian wife and learn how to submit and how to love my husband. I remember I was sitting there at the kitchen table playing with my toys, and I did not know what was going on. I know as a kid you may have your imaginary friend, so that is who I thought I was talking to. I went to my grandmother and told her all about what God had spoken over me, because I was a kid. My granny said, "That is so cute," and I said, "He did say that to me, Granny!" But I don't think she believed me. I said, "Granny, I am going to get married one day and be so happy." I was telling Tyrone that I truly believed that God was speaking over me at the age of seven, and I was standing there looking at him knowing that God had been talking about him. I hugged him for the first time. It was a big hug, and I kissed him on his cheek and he kissed me on my cheek. Now remember we both were practicing celibacy, and so this was the most we had touched.

My son was so happy for me because he could see how

happy I was. We went to breakfast and then we went to his church. When we got to the restaurant, I kept looking down at my ring. Now if I can take you back to when we went on the second date and Tyrone had the magazine with the rings in it. He'd asked me to pick out the ring that I would like when I got married. At that time, I had told him about the $400 ring that was in the magazine. The ring that I had looked at then was worth more than I ever imagined, and it was beautiful. I thought I was dreaming because I could picture me being married to my King. So, all that morning Tyrone and I were so happy. He was smiling showing all teeth, and I was smiling so much that I could not even eat my breakfast. We left the restaurant and we were heading to his church, Deliverance Mission Christian Church (DMCC).

When we got to the church, everybody knew Minister Tyrone. I did not realize he had been there for over 14 years. He said that he started out working on the parking lot and then he moved to cleaning the church. Pastor Monty ordained him, and he was the only Deacon at church at that time. He started telling me this as we are walking into the church. I said, "You have been here and serving for a long time!" The church members were so friendly. Tyrone introduced me as his fiancé and told them that we were going to be getting married in seven months. Tyrone then told me that he wanted me to meet somebody who was special to him. I agreed to meet the person and asked who it was, and he told me that it was the person who had saved his life, Pastor Monty Weatherall. Tyrone took me back to the Pastor's office before the church service to meet him. It was nice meeting all the church members and the Pastor. I met over four hundred members that day and everybody was so nice to me and my son. Some of the members that I met were telling me how blessed I was to get married to Minister Tyrone. Pastor Monty Weatherall was nice, and he seemed like he was very happy to meet me. I found myself visiting his church once a month and I enjoyed the service. I always wanted my husband and I to fellowship at the same church and even though I know other couples that attend different churches, I just believe a husband and wife should fellowship at the same church. I thought it was important for us to get the same teaching. When I was growing up, my father would always say that the man is the head of the household. He should lead, and the wife should follow her husband. That is the principle that my father as a pastor taught us as children, and I believe it stuck with me.

Before going any further, I want to tell you more about my husband. I want to tell you a little of his story. Elder Howard Tyrone Thorpe was a native of East Saint Louis, Illinois. He began his Christian journey about 20 years ago after spending several years of his life blind to the ways of Jesus and his amazing grace. Elder Howard Tyrone Thorpe boasted that he was "once hooked on crack but now he was hooked on Jesus!" In 1998, he came to know the Lord and joined Deliverance Mission Christian Church (DMCC), where he devotedly served as the janitor, parking lot attendant, and then

Sunday school teacher. Always willing to put the work in first, his years of servitude continued when he was ordained as a Deacon in 2001 and later as a Minister in 2007. In 2010, Elder Tyrone was certified by the prestigious International Association of Biblical Counseling. He received his Associate Degree at Gateway Biblical Counseling and Training Center. He provided pastoral counseling and accepted other duties which include, visiting the sick, counseling married and premarital couples, and baptizing new converts. He also led the Keeping in Touch [K.I.T.] Ministry. Simply put, Elder Tyrone would faithfully do whatever was needed to advance the Kingdom of God. Elder Tyrone received his ordination as Elder in June of 2013, which entitled him to all privileges granted to a person of the cloth. He was entrusted to perform all duties in ministry, including marriage and biblical discipline, just to name a few. Elder Tyrone stood on the principle that his life is a testimony of what Jesus can do for you. I just wanted to provide a bit more information about my husband, and his story, so you will know who he was. Tyrone was indeed a great man of God. That is the man God blessed me with, and the man God had prepared me for.

When I got back to work, I started talking with some of my co-workers who knew Tyrone. Tyrone was very well-known at the VA hospital since he had worked there for over 34 years. I was also sharing with one co-worker that Tyrone proposed to me, and I also let the young lady who had introduced us know what had happened. She was so happy for me. Two of his co-workers were talking to me, telling me how blessed I was to be getting married to him. They also told me that he had been praying for a wife for over seven years and that he been through a lot with drugs and alcohol, but God had healed him and set him free. One of the nurses that I worked with at the VA hospital told me she was concerned about me. She told me she was concerned because we hadn't known each other long and it seemed like we were very serious. I told her yes, we were very serious, and we would be getting married on June 11, 2011. I told her we realized it was only 7 months that we'd known each other. She asked me what his name was and said she probably knew him. I told her that he worked in the kitchen and he was a supervisor, and his name was Howard Tyrone Thorpe. She said, "Oh I know him! He is a Christian man and helps everybody." She shared with me that she and my fiancé would talk all time, and that she would give him fresh sage out of her garden. Tyrone and I would always say to people who didn't understand why we were getting married after only knowing each other for seven months that one day is like a thousand year unto the Lord. Every time I would see him I would just be so happy, and he would be smiling at me. I told him that I was dreaming, and he told me the dream was real. I can truly say that he didn't come selling the dream; he came with the dream.

I know that Tyrone was everything that I had been praying for; he knew that I was everything that he had prayed for, and I know that God had ordained our marriage. Tyrone and I began to talk about me moving back to Illinois. I was living in Saint Louis and I was purchasing this home as a rent to own purchase. The plans were for us to purchase a new home. I was going to move into it with my son, and Tyrone would move in when we got married. He already had a home, and he remained in it until after the wedding. So, we started looking for new homes while I was still planning my wedding. While we were discussing the plans for the wedding, I got a phone call from my landlord telling me she would release me from rent to own agreement, but I would have to pay an early termination fee. Tyrone was with me when I got the phone call, and he told me that we would pay the remaining balance because we were under contract on the home we were planning to buy in Illinois.

Every night and every morning we were praying over the plans that we were asking of God for the wedding and for our marriage. I found a tenant to takeover my lease and it happened so quickly, that I now did not have anywhere to stay because we had not closed on the new house yet. My fiancé called me and told me had some good news: he was willing to move out of his house and move into a hotel for two and a half months and let my son and I stay in his home. His niece called him that day and after he mentioned what was going on, she offered to let him move in with her until we closed on the house. However, there was a problem with our financing because they checked my credit and told us that I had to work on cleaning up my credit in order for them to approve us for the loan. They said it would take about four years before they could approve a loan for us. One of my girlfriends told me about a real estate agency that worked with people who had low credit scores and helped people get approved for home loans. This was a program through the VA that we went with, and we were approved for the loan for our home in about two months. We were so happy and felt so blessed that God worked out a miracle to allow us to purchase our home that we would share together after we were married.

Even though both of us had been married twice before, we felt like this was the first Holy marriage for both of us that had the Blessing of God. We both had been celibate, and we had been saving ourselves for the person God had for us. I know that it was truly a blessing that I was celibate for over eight years, and that when God sent me the husband he had for me, he had been celibate for seven years. I never met a man who was so real and honest about his relationship with God. Prior to our wedding day, we both started a 30-day fast that we did while we were going through counseling with our Pastor for our marriage to be blessed.

Tyrone and I had discussed having a King and Queen wedding. I wanted to crown him as my King and he accepted me as his Queen. My girlfriend and I planned to have lunch and she was going to help me shop for my wedding dress. Before we left, there was a knock at the door and it was Tyrone with a dozen roses and his big Kool-Aid smile. He said, "My love, I knew you were going to lunch with your girlfriend to look for your wedding dress, and I did not want you to worry about the money to pay for the dress." He presented me with a check and it was for $1000. He wanted me to use it to buy the dress of my dreams. He left, and my girlfriend and I went shopping for my wedding dress at David's Bridal Shop. When I went in the store, we were greeted at the door and the sales person told us it was a good day because they had dresses on clearance and on sale. I tried on three dresses, one was on clearance and the other two were on sale. I tried on the two dresses that were on sale first and they fit, but they were not my dream dress. I tried on the clearance dress and I just burst in tears in the shop because it was my dream dress and it fit perfectly. I looked at the price tag and it was $5000, but when I got to the cash register, the clerk told me the dress was on clearance for $1000, which was the exact amount of the check my fiancé had given me to purchase my dream dress. I was excited, and I was crying and very emotional and I asked the clerk if she could give me a minute. I got out of line and went to call my fiancé to tell him how excited I was because not only did I find the dress of my dreams, but he had given the exact amount I needed to be able to purchase my it. I thanked him, and he said, "My love, you have not seen anything yet. The best is yet to come." Before I checked out, the clerk showed me the head pieces and I chose one that was the perfect match to my dress. I didn't want to leave my dress there, but she told me I needed to because they needed to make some small alterations and add the hook to the dress that I would use to hook up the train on the dress while I danced at my reception. They told me the dress would be ready to pick up in two weeks which was great because that was two months before my wedding day.

Later that evening, Tyrone and I sat down with our wedding coordinator to go over the arrangements for the wedding. We were pleased with the arrangements and the price and agreed to hire her as our wedding coordinator. We left there and went to the bakery to meet with the wedding cake baker because we had an appointment to do the cake tasting. It went well, and we were pleased with price and taste of the cake. We'd had two other cake tasting appointments, however we decided to go with the first bakery. Three days later, we met with the photographer who was going to photograph our wedding. We took pictures for our Save the Date reminders.

We were required to attend marriage counseling before the wedding and it was conducted by Pastor Monty Weatherall. Marriage counseling consisted of four sessions, and we attended one each week. Minister Tyrone was a marriage counselor however, he felt it was important for us to attend marriage counseling. Our pastor wanted to address some things because we had both been married twice before, and he wanted to discuss some things that he thought would be important in our marriage and blended families. I thank God for Pastor Monty for the counseling sessions that we received before we got married. I thanked him for him talking about the blended family because my son was very close to his dad, and it was just me and Malcolm for over eight years. Malcolm liked Tyrone, but there was still a part of him that hoped his dad and me would get back together. Pastor Monty also mentioned that he would like to do communion with us. We were so excited that he mentioned it because we wanted to take communion in front everyone.

The wedding ceremony was going to begin at 1:00 pm. I was so excited and before it was time for me to walk down the aisle. My son came over to talk to me. He told me he was very excited for me. He said he was happy I was getting married, and he thought Mr. Tyrone was a good man and he liked him. He told me that he wished I would have given him the opportunity to sit down with the pastor, Mr. Tyrone and me. He told me he had concerns about how me getting married was going to change our relationship. I told Malcolm we didn't realize how he was feeling and I was sorry that we didn't get a chance to have him in a counseling session with us and the Pastor. The pastor had talked to us about blended families and how it was so important for us agree with one another. Malcolm told me he just wanted me to know how he was feeling, because he was getting emotional. He knew that I was getting ready to get married and he felt like he was losing me since I was now getting married to Mr. Tyrone. It was now becoming real to him as we got closer to the time for the wedding, and so he felt sad and happy at the same time. Malcolm told me he loved me, and he prayed that everything worked out with my new husband. My son was 16 years old when Tyrone and I got married. He asked me if I was ready to walk down the aisle. I said yes. He told me I looked beautiful and gave me a kiss on the right side of my cheek.

I was so excited that day, and I truly felt like a Queen. The doors opened, and I saw a lot of flashes as everybody was talking pictures of me and Malcolm; everyone was smiling and looking at me. I said to myself, "I'm not going to cry, because I have waited eight years for this marriage. This is one of the happiest moments of my life. I am about to marry my king, and I'm going to focus my attention on my fiancé." As I was coming down aisle, the song, *I Give Myself Away*, by William McDowell was playing. I was so happy that God had blessed me with my king, and when I looked up at him, he had on his crown and it fit him like a king. He was dancing and happy. Everyone who knew Tyrone, knew he was a happy man and he loved praising God. As I got up to the front, the song just kept repeating, "I give myself away, so you Lord can use me." The pastor asked, "Who gives this woman to be married?" and Malcolm said, "I do." Then the Pastor said to Minister Tyrone, "Go get your bride." I looked around the room and there were over 300 people in the church. There were people standing up on both sides of the room and in the back. I forget to mention that before my husband and I got married I had joined church with my husband because I just felt like it would be good to join church and fellowship with my husband before we got married. I remember the day I joined, Tyrone ran up to me and said what are you doing? He asked me if I was joining his church and I told him yes, it was put on my heart to join DMCC today and he was so happy.

The pastor prayed over us before he did the wedding service and right after that, Tyrone and I lit the unity candle. My husband and I wanted to present flowers to his sisters and to my dad and granddad, and once we get back on the stage,

Pastor Monty proceeded with the wedding. He talked to us about keeping God first, having God to be the center of our marriage, and keeping our family and friends out of our marriage. He also mentioned how we waited to save ourselves until after we were married. The pastor continued with the ceremony, and right before we did the exchange of the rings, he prayed over us again. Tyrone and I had written our own vows, and we said our vows to one another. This was Tyrone's vow:

"God, you, and me. I am going to build my whole world around God, you and me. Our love will be pure victory. We will be more than a conqueror in this life. God has made you my wife. I pray that God will take a drop of rain and wash away all your pain. Each day I pray for the love of God you and me will stay, for true love can never fly away, but it grows stronger each day. This is God's way. Because He made love to stay, I will love you always even in the worst of days. Our love will pass the test, because our love is the very best-oiled is God and God is love, from heaven up above. The sweet Holy Spirit lives inside of us, therefore we are about to burst, because we have a powerful thirst. God, you, and me. Alisha Thorpe will you marry me? June 11th, God 's love will fall from Heaven. I love you today. I will love you tomorrow. I loved you yesterday, my love is here to stay. God, you, and me. Our love will never flee, because we have the Victory."

These are the vows I wrote to Tyrone:

"Forever Love (Genesis 2: 22-24). Tyrone, as God gave Eve to Adam to become his helper, I believe that God has placed the two of us in each other's lives, so we could help each other grow in His love. In the time that I have known you, you have done so much more than help me. You have inspired me, taught me, even enlightened me. My days with you I believe are like what days must be like in God's Heaven. I love you, Tyrone, and I promise to be more than just your helpmate in the faith, but also to be your lover, your steadfast supporter, the provider of your needs, and your best friend. I promise to love you and cherish you, to respect and protect you for as long as I live, regardless of the obstacles or challenges that come our way, until death do us part.

Thank you, God, for my husband Tyrone Thorpe."

And then the pastor prayed over us again and we did the exchange of the rings. We didn't just have a wedding; we could truly say God showed up and showed out - we had church. My husband broke out right after the vows. He said, "No more pain, no more heartaches, no more suffering." He was set free; the chains had been broken off, for I can truly say we both were feeling happy and free. The Pastor said to Tyrone, "You may kiss your bride," and my husband kissed me and kept on kissing me. The fact that we had been celibate made us anxious to be alone and we could not wait for the wedding to be over with, but you know we had to go to the reception.

We didn't want to stay to long, but we stayed for about

two to three hours. My husband had surprised me at the reception with a carriage ride with two white horses; it was so beautiful and romantic. My husband was all about surprises. He told me that he had tried to surprise me by having butterflies released but the wedding coordinator couldn't get them. We had a beautiful reception and we were celebrating will all our family and friends. We had invited 350 people to the reception and everyone was coming up to Tyrone and me saying how beautiful the wedding was and that they had never been to wedding like this before. We both looked at each other and started laughing. We said that we know, because God was all in this. I am telling you Tyrone was truly my best friend and even though we didn't know each other for a long time before we got married, we truly were soulmates. We had a spiritual connection that neither of us had ever had before and it was a wonderful thing.

We stayed at the reception for about three hours and then we stood up and thanked everyone for coming to help us celebrate our love, for all the beautiful gifts, and for the contributions to the wishing well.

Tyrone and I left the reception to begin our honeymoon and our wedding coordinator had made reservations for us at a hotel. We were staying in the honeymoon suite. It was so beautiful, and it had a Jacuzzi in the middle of the room. My husband was so happy when we got to the honeymoon suite and he saw how big and beautiful it was. He said, "Now this is what I'm talking about! A big Jet Jacuzzi. You see my love, years ago I was homeless for about four years and I couldn't even take a bath, so I am grateful to be able to take a bath in a tub." Tyrone and I stayed at the hotel for two days and we really enjoyed each other and honeymoon suite.

We woke up on Sunday morning and we started talking about our life and the things that we wanted to do. My king first started out with prayer, and he told me we must always keep God in the center of our marriage. He also told me that he wanted me to work side by side with him as he continued his worked in the ministry. Before my husband and I got married, he was already counseling couples and performing pre-marital counseling, and he said that he wanted me to start sitting in the sessions with him. I thanked him for allowing me to be involved in his ministry, and I was so excited to be doing it with him. I told him I believed that we both believed in marriage and people staying together, and I also told him that there are scriptures that tells us to stay together in the Bible. That's why we must keep the Word of God in our heart and in everything we do. It is a good road map for a marriage and it can help prevent many divorces and separations. My husband's heart was so big, and he loved helping couples save their marriage. We also talked about our marriage and how we wanted to keep prayer in our home.

My husband always loved to surprise me with gifts and he told me he had a big surprise for me. He was so excited, and he felt that I would be just as excited when he told me his good news. The surprise was that we had been approved for the house we had been praying to God for. My husband told me that when we came back from our honeymoon, we would be able to close on the house and move in together. Suddenly, Tyrone jumped up and said, "I forgot to give our tithes to Pastor Monty at the reception!" He said as soon as we got dressed we needed to go back to the church to pay our tithes. My husband was very faithful when it came to God. We pulled up to the church and our Pastor was outside greeting the members as they were walking into the church. The Pastor had a big smile on his face when he saw us pull up and he asked us what we were doing here and said that we were supposed to be on our honeymoon. We were going to Florida for a week for our honeymoon, and I would meet his daughter while we were there. My husband said, "Pastor, we forgot to give you our tithes and we wanted to drop it off before we left town."

We went to breakfast and while we were eating, Tyrone and I talked about me meeting his only daughter. He told me that he loved her so much, but when he was out there on drugs, he didn't get a chance to spend time with his daughter and that he missed out on so many years of her life. Tyrone told me when his daughter got older she came to visit him, and they got a chance to get close and form a real father and daughter relationship. He said, "When you meet her, just be yourself. She's going to love you because she is going to see the love you have for me." I was excited to meet his only daughter because he had met my kids, but I had never met his daughter. He talked about her all the time and what a good relationship they had now. He said he told her she can have all the degrees and he certainly encouraged her to get an education, but the most important thing she needed to have was a relationship with God. He said he told her that's the best and for her to get know God.

We just spent the rest of the day loving on one another. We were so happy, and I kept looking at him saying, "It feels like a dream, but I know that it's true." Monday morning, we woke up and headed to the airport to catch our plane to Florida. We would be spending seven days in Orlando, Florida, and we would be staying in the honeymoon suite at the Hampton Inn. The honeymoon suite was very nice; we were able to look out over the hotel from our balcony. The next day his daughter and her husband drove up to meet us and we went out to eat. I was so nervous when I met his daughter, but we got along very well, and I was so happy to meet her. We had a good time, and his son-in-law was nice. They told me they were so happy to meet me, and they were glad that their dad had met someone. His daughter told me that as long as her dad was happy, she was happy and that we made a good couple. The next day we planned to go to *Holy Land*, which is a theater that shows plays about the Bible. We had a wonderful time and it was like the bible stories came alive during the play.

We returned home from Florida the following Monday and the rest of the week we spent packing as we prepared to move into our new home. My husband and I went to look for new furniture because he said that he wanted to get all new furniture for our new home. We went into the furniture store and as soon as we walked in, we saw this beautiful bedroom set that had a canopy bed. I had always wanted to have a canopy bed, and he was looking at me when he said, "My love I have always wanted to have a bed like this." I told him I loved it as well, and we bought the bedroom set. Tyrone still had his first house up for sale but after a few months went by, we decided not to sell it. We decided to advertise it in the paper as a rental, and we could find a good tenant and have that as extra income. Everything was going so well, and we were so happy and in love.

My husband decided the next year to come off his job on disability. The disability occurred when my husband was in the army; his feet were injured, and they had to do surgery on both his feet. During the surgery, they cut too much of the bone out of his toes, and it has caused him a lot of pain all the time. My husband had worked over 30 years, which included active military service, reserve service, and service as a government employee. He was so looking forward to retiring but he came out two months before his retirement on disability. His disability did not stop him from getting out though, it just allowed him to get closer to God. My husband had a hard time dealing with the fact that he had to come off his job and receive disability, but I told him he couldn't look at it as a bad thing. I said that it was a blessing that he was still able to walk. He did not even have any feeling in his toes. I said, "A lot of people have disabilities; it doesn't stop them, and it won't stop you." I had to encourage my husband because the enemy will try to tell you that things are hopeless or that they are worse than they are, and so I would encourage my king every day. I said, "Honey, God created YOU and made you and just because you had to come off your job two months before your retirement on disability does not make you any less deserving of what you are receiving. We must give God all the praise." I could see the change in how my husband looked at the situation and suddenly he began to praise God. One day, before we had gotten married, I was over to his house and he said he wanted to show me something, and he prayed that I would still love him after I saw it. He pulled off both of his socks and showed me his feet. When I looked at his toes they looked like baby toes. He said I pray that you will still love me and I told him that I would love him forever and that I was not marrying his toes, I was marrying him. I told him no matter what, we are going to be married to until death do us part. He grabbed me and hugged me and kissed me (I forgot that we weren't supposed to kiss because we were not married yet ☺). I'm telling you everything was still looking up. We were still loving on each other and enjoying the life we were starting to build together.

In 2011, my husband had been telling me that he wanted me to get out of the car I was driving because it was giving me so many problems. One day, my husband came up to my job with a new car that he had bought for me, so he asked me to come outside to see it. When I came, out he pulled up with a big smile on his face in a brand new 2011 Kia Soul. He said, "My love, do you love your new car?" I told himyes, and he said this would also help my credit and that we were going to rebuild my credit. He said I'm also going to teach you how to live by the 10/10 /80 principle: ten percent to God, ten percent to savings, and 80 percent to our bills. I told him that sounded like a good plan and I would be willing to learn. So, my husband leaves with the car to go back to the dealership to finish all the paperwork. It was my very first brand new car and I was so grateful for it.

There was something special about that year 2011. We got married, we moved into our new home, and I got a new car. I was so in love with my husband and I kept thanking God every day for dropping him down from heaven, because in my heart, I felt that he was heaven sent. In 2012, I gave my husband a retirement party for being with the VA hospital for over 30 years. He was so surprised, and when he walked in the first thing he wanted to know was how much all this cost! My husband never wanted me to spend money on him, but he always wanted to spend money on me. We had this game that we played where we always tried to beat each other being good to each other. Right after that, Tyrone's birthday came around and he was turning 55 years old. I was going to give him 55 birthday cards and it took me three months to find all the cards that said what I wanted them to say. I'm telling you, we were still so happy and we said this is too good to be true, but we knew that God put us together.

After I was delivered from my pain and depression, God began to increase me greatly – He began to grow me! He blessed me to donate a kidney; He blessed me with a new job. But the biggest blessing of all was how all those things led me to my soulmate, the love of my life, my husband Tyrone. Growth is God's way of letting us know that we can't stay in the last place. Especially with sadness and depression, we are not ready or equipped to receive the abundance of blessings God has for us. I could never have been the loving wife I was to Tyrone if I had still been in a place of fear and anxiety. He could have never been the husband he was if he'd never been delivered from his issues. Our bliss together was our sign that God was growing us up in Him in new and amazing ways.

When I began to focus on God, my children, and my purpose, God began to bless me! I would pray, "God, I want all you have to give me." One thing I would say to anyone going through something is to continue to pray. The key is keeping your eyes on what you want to achieve, and you can have everything that you want in life. Even though I went through trials and tribulation, I didn't stop because they made me stronger. I didn't give up because I knew that God had a purpose for me and I know he has a purpose for you also if you only believe.

Reflections

Questions

1. Think back to your childhood. Think about what you are good at, the things you loved doing. Reflect in the next few pages on how using what's inside of you could help your family, your community, our world?

2. We all were born to accomplish something specific. There's something that you can do that nobody else can do like YOU. What is that? What is your purpose in life? Do you believe you are on the road to growing and fulfilling it?

3. Maybe you can't give a kidney, but there's something (growing) inside of you that you can give the world. What is that? Is it your voice?

Reflections

Reflections

Reflections

Reflections

4
GOODNESS

With all the joy and bliss I had experienced after I was delivered from my depression, losing my husband could have put me right back in that place. After all, Tyrone was the love of my life, the husband God had promised me at the age of seven. It was very hard to understand why he would now be taken away so swiftly. But because of what I had come through, I was slowly able to understand that going back to that place of sadness was not an option. God had simply been too good.

I was at the top of my game! I was in love like I never had experienced before. I was a faithful Christian. Did most of the right things, had experienced turmoil, but was finally experiencing my best life. Yet, suddenly, my king had left! My fairytale had ended! How could God do this to me?! How?!

As you can see, after my husband passed away, I had so many questions for God. My first question was, "What is my purpose here? You took my husband and left me here!" The second question was, "What am I going to do without my husband?" We were so in love and did everything together. I told God that I had found true happiness and that I had met my soul mate, and I needed help understanding why and how it was suddenly gone. But God had answers for my questions.

God showed us in the Bible how our earthly body would get sick and we would pass away, but we would have a new body in heaven. He also told me that to be absent from the body is to be present with Him. God gave me comfort by letting me know that Tyrone was not dead; he was just resting and I will see him again. It was like God was right there in my bedroom talking to me and I felt so much comfort and so much love from my Father that night. The next morning, I woke up and he told me that he was birthing out of me a book. He wanted me to write a book about my life and the pain that I was going through. God told me that I would be able to write it in 90 days. He told me he would be sending me help to get it completed and that so many lives would be changed because of it. He said, **You will be able to tell my people how you are going from grief to goodness.** He told me how I would be able to tell my testimony and how it would help others cope with their grief. That morning I was almost overwhelmed because it was so much to take in, and I knew that I was hearing from God.

Right after my husband passed away, I could not remember anything. I was forgetting so much and though I could remember the date we had got married, I could not even picture me walking down the aisle on our wedding day. I was trying to remember so many good times that we had together, but it was like my mind had gone blank. God told me the reason I couldn't remember was because he wanted me to save it all for the book that was going to be written. **The goodness is I have faith in God, in all He has done for me; when He died on the cross for me, he took all my sickness and sin so that I would be able to go on.**

God is my healer, my restorer, my strength, my deliverer, my resting place, my lover, my friend, my husband, my everlasting father, my stronghold, my hiding place, the Lord who provides, the Lord of peace, my wonderful Counselor, my helper, my hope, my refuge from the storm, and my eternal life. This is what he has been to me in midst of my husband's illness and his passing away. If I didn't have God, the Pastor's teaching, and my family and friends, I could not get through this. Before Tyrone passed, I talked with him and told him that I released him, and he could go home to be with the Father. My husband did not want any sadness at his homegoing service. He had written his own eulogy and our Pastor Monty Weatherall preached it exactly as it was written. I can truly say we had a homegoing service and on that day, fourteen people gave their life to the Lord. I know Tyrone was smiling down from Heaven with that big Kool-Aid smile. ☺

Still, I was very lost and did not know how I was going to be able to pick the pieces and go on without the love of my life, my King. I was on leave from my job from November 2016 until June 2017, and I was so blessed to have such wonderful co-workers who helped me by donating leave time that allowed me to be off with pay after I had exhausted all my leave. I was even blessed with a week of leave time from a doctor and a chaplain on my job.

The goodness I have been receiving is the love from so many of my church members and my teacher of the Word, Pastor Monty Weatherall. Right after I laid my husband to rest, my great- niece and nephew and my best friend's granddaughter who I consider my niece also, all came to me and told me they wanted to start a praise team in honor of my husband. They said they knew he was man of faith and he was always preaching about love. I was just listening to them, and they were saying that they believed this would help me heal. They said that they had decided on a name for the team and it would be Ministry Teen; the bible verses they wanted to use were 1 Corinthians 13:4-8. It sounded like they had it all planned out. They said they had one more request and that was to ask me to be the manager and for my sister to be the assistant manager. I told them to let me pray about it, and a week later I called them and told them yes, I would be honored to manage them. I didn't know this was part of my healing, it just seemed as if God was just sending all kinds of help to comfort me. Two months later my family and friends came over to celebrate

Tyrone's and my six-year anniversary. We were just sitting around talking about the love of my life Tyrone. I can't remember who asked me the question of what they could do to let me know that they would be here for me. I said I was glad I was asked the question, because I felt like after Tyrone passed away, so many of the phone calls had stopped and people stopped coming by to check on me. I didn't want anybody else to feel that way, so my request was that I would like to get together once a month to just love on one another and show love to each other. I felt that would help me heal and allow me to share the goodness of God with so many women. We named the group Faith, Family, and Friends, and we started our first ladies group in July of 2017. It is still going strong, and we are up to about 45 women who come out to fellowship and show love to one another. It was put on my heart that every woman who holds a monthly meeting for me will be blessed with a gift from God. I can truly say it has really been a blessing, and all the women come out to love on me and one another. I know that's God.

At one of the gatherings at my home, my sister-in-law who had recently joined my church and rededicated her life to the Lord, was asking questions about Bible study and I told her about groups that would be starting soon at the church. She was hungry for the Word and eager to learn, and God put it on my heart to start a Bible study group at my home. This would fill the need I saw to minister to one of His children. I started a weekly Bible study at my home using the lesson plan of the Fruits of the Spirit, which lasted nine weeks. At the end of nine weeks it was a successful group; testimonies were being shared and we were growing in the Lord. The sister-in-law is now holding the Bible study at her home, and I am so glad that I heard the need and answered the call. To God be the glory! I have been blessed to have been put in the right places at the right time to help people and to minister to people. The other blessing in all of this is that we are all being a blessing to each other, and it helped me so much during my time of grief. Even through my grief, I was surrounded by goodness and I was able to be good to someone else.

I can truly say that since my husband has gone home to be with the Lord, I've been so busy doing the work of God that it has really been helping with my healing. Don't get me wrong: I miss my husband dearly, and the hardest time for me is at night time when I get off work and go home. But when I'm at home, I feel the peace of God in my home and I feel my husband's presence. I can't stop thanking my sister who has been so much a part of my life since my husband's illness and passing and I thank God for bringing us closer together. Since my husband passed away, my wonderful sisters and I have gotten so much closer and have a great relationship today. That has been my prayer since we were little kids when my sisters and I lived apart. Family is everything to me, and my prayer has always been for my family to be saved and that they would have eternal life with Jesus. Now it is happening in front of my eyes! I have been praying for this for over ten years and it's happening right now. Over fifteen members of my family have become saved or rededicated their live back to God, and four of them have gotten baptized. I give all the praise to God. My grandfather who is 94 years old even gave his life to the Lord. I remember when my husband and I went to Chicago to bring him back home to Saint Louis. My grandfather was sick, and I asked my husband if we could bring him back to take care of him and he said yes. That made me so happy because I believe it was our responsibility to take care of our grandfather. So, my baby sister and I agreed to take care of him. He is so much healthier now; he is able to live by himself at 94 years old We go by and check on him and my sister and I take care of him. I take care of all his important business and order all his medication. This is another part of my healing, to be able to take care of my grandfather while he is still alive.

I want to mention that in 2007 my daughter graduated from high school. She was accepted at Southern Illinois University- Carbondale. She attended there for four years and graduated with a bachelor's degree in criminal justice and a minor in mortuary science. I am so proud of Davida, and what she achieved. She's now back in school, working on her second bachelor's degree as a human resource recruiter. She is also raising her son as a single mother but is doing well for herself. She's spending a lot of time with God and building a strong relationship with him. My daughter is a full-time student and is working full time and working for *Blue Cross Blue Shield* as an insurance representative and she has training experience in management. I am also proud of my son Malcolm; he graduated from high school and he is doing well. My son first job was working at Target and part-time at Wendy's. He worked those jobs until he was about 18 years old. When Malcolm turned 19, he became a manager at FedEx. He worked for FedEx until he was 21 years old. Malcolm signed up for military service on my birthday. I will never forget February 2, 2018. My daughter that I gained through my marriage to Tyrone, Veronica, is doing amazing! We have bonded greatly, and our relationship is thriving, especially after the passing of my husband, her father. Even my very first husband, my ex-husband, is now an avid believer and follower of Christ our Savior and Redeemer. Currently, he is happily married to his wife of 13 years and doing well. I have forgiven him and we, along with Tyrone, maintained a respectable friendship throughout the years.

Though I've gone through some struggles and road blocks, it did not stop me or my children. They are all doing well, and I am so proud of them. I thank God, each day for trusting me with them, God has truly delivered, covered and blessed all of us.

I want to end this book with some scriptures that have helped me on this journey from grief to goodness. I want to provide you, the reader, with some reminders that no matter what you're going through, no matter how hard life gets, God is still good, and He is still with you. He still loves you, and He still plans to take care of you. I know, for it is my own testimony, that God can deliver you out of any snare. Keep believing in Him and His Word, keep praying, and keep moving into all that God has for you!

THE WAY TO LOVE

Love is patient and kind; love does not envy or boast; it is not arrogant or rude. It does not insist on its own way; it is not irritable or resentful; it does not rejoice at wrong doing but rejoices with the truth. Love bears all things, believes all things, hopes all things, endures all things. Love never ends. As for prophecies, they will pass away; as for tongues, they will cease; as for knowledge, it will pass away. 1 Corinthians 13:4-8

God's Love: 1 Thessalonians 3:12

God's understanding: 1 Peter 3:7

Your value to God: Prov 31:10

Hope: Jeremiah 29:11

Trust: 1 John 4:18

Respect: Ephesians 5:33

Submission: Ephesians 5:21

Kindness: Proverbs: 31: 26

Purpose: Romans 8:28

PRAYER FOR COMFORT

Though we may realize our faith is most strengthened, not in the easy times of life, but in the most trying, it's often hard to walk that out once we're swirling in the midst of it all. We long for carefree days, yet sometimes, God takes our hand and leads us straight into the darkest of times. Not to harm us, ever, but to bring greater strength, character, trust, beauty, and perseverance to the deepest part of our souls.

RECOVERING FROM GRIEF

"He heals the brokenhearted and binds up their wounds." (Ps. 147:3)

"Blessed be God, the Father of our Lord Jesus Christ, the Father of mercies, and the God of all comfort, who comforts us in all our tribulation, that we may be able to comfort those who are in any trouble by the comfort with which we ourselves are comforted by God." (2 Cor. 1:3-4)

"Do not fear, for I am with you; do not be dismayed, for I am your God. I will strengthen you, I will help you, yes, and I will uphold you with my righteous right hand." (Is. 41:10)

"But he said to me, 'My grace is sufficient for you, for my power is made perfect in weakness." Therefore, I will boast all the more gladly of my weaknesses, so that the power of Christ may rest upon me." (2 Cor. 12:9)

My prayer for those who are grieving today. I ask for your comfort to surround those who weep. I pray for the peace of your presence to cover your minds and thoughts, as God covers us. The enemy can never steal us out of his hands. He never has the final say over our lives. We are kept safe in His presence forever, whether in life or in death. That is God's Promise to us.

Dear God,

Some days it too hard. We're hurting. Struggling. Fighting fear and worry at every turn. Thank you for being in the midst of it all, you haven't left us to fend for ourselves. Forgive us for doubting you are there. Forgive us for thinking you've forgotten. Forgive us for believing we somehow know the better way and you fully trustworthy. You are All Powerful. You are Able. You are Lord over every situation no matter how difficult it may seem. You are a Healer and will never waste the grief we carry today. You will use all things for good in some way. Anything is possible with you. Nothing is too hard or difficult for you.

Revelation 21:3-4

Psalm 147: 3
Matthew 5:4
Ecclesiastes 3:1-4
John 14: 1
Numbers 23:19-21

2 Corinthians 1:3 -4
Luke 12:22-26
Romans 8:38-39
Matthews 6:34
Joshua 1:9

Mark 6:50
Psalm 118:6-7
Psalm 91:1-16
Zephaniah 3:17

"But he gives more grace. Therefore, it says, "God opposes the proud, but gives grace to the humble." (James 4:6)

Blessed be God, the Father of our Lord Jesus Christ, the Father of mercies, and the God of all comfort, who comforts us in all our tribulation, that we may be able to comfort those who are in any trouble by the comfort with which we ourselves are comforted by God." (2 Cor. 1:3-4)

Do not fear, for I am with you; do not be dismayed, for I am your God. I will strengthen you, I will help you, yes, I will uphold you with My righteous right hand." (Is. 41:10)

"He himself bore our sins in his body on the tree, that we might die to sin and live to righteousness. By his wounds you have been healed." (1 Pet. 2:24)

"Cast your burden on the Lord, and he will sustain you; he will never permit the righteous to be moved." (Ps. 55:22)

"Come to me, all who labor and are heavy laden, and I will give you rest. Take my yoke upon you, and learn from me, for I am gentle and lowly in heart, and you will find rest for your souls. For my yoke is easy, and my burden is light." (Matt. 11:28-30)

"But he said to me, "My grace is sufficient for you, for my power is made perfect in weakness." Therefore, I will boast all the more gladly of my weaknesses, so that the power of Christ may rest upon me." (2 Cor. 12:9)

OVERCOMING FEAR & ANXIETY

Fear is one of the enemy's most popular weapons that he uses against us. Worry, anxiety, and fear can overwhelm us with a thick shadow of darkness, controlling our every move and decision.

So much craziness is going on around us today - wars, conflicts, persecution, violence, crime, natural disasters, terrorism, economic uncertainty, unemployment, divisions, diseases like cancer, high blood pressure, diabetes, heart disease, and kidney failure. We fear death, we fear for our children's future, we fear for our families, we fear for our financial future, we fear for our safety. The list goes on... and is long. There actually is a lot we could potentially worry about. Yet reality tells us that so much of what we spend our time worrying about never even happens. Living under the weight of the "what if's" is a hard place to dwell.

I struggled with fear and worry for years, but over time, I began to put my trust and hope in the Lord and that is what got me through.

Questions

1. Sometimes when grief is presence, we are blinded from the blesses.

2. Define grace. Recount instances during your life when you knew God's grace was presence?

3. How do have remain encouraged during difficult seasons of your life?

Reflections

Reflections

Reflections

Reflections

SPECIAL INTERVIEW ABOUT TYRONE

There are some men whom you meet for the first time, and you just know they will become a great and forever friend. Such was our introduction to Pastor Tyrone Thorpe and his wife Alisha in 2014 at a marriage seminar in East St. Louis, Illinois.

Cathy and I were invited along with our wonderful friend, Carolyn Lilley, to assist in a marriage seminar to strengthen believers at 15th Street Baptist Church in East St. Louis. Carolyn, Cathy and I are members of First Baptist Church in Branson, Missouri, and our church has had a missions relationship with 15th Street Baptist and their pastor Andrew Prowell for at least 10 years. We had done 2 marriage seminars in previous years in their church and were proposing to make this teaching seminar an annual event. At this particular seminar Pastor Prowell's brother, Tyrone Thorpe and his wife Alisha were in attendance, and we were introduced. At the time Tyrone was serving as Deacon in another church, and he and Alisha were not regular attendees at 15th Street Baptist.

Several personal qualities Cathy and I immediately noticed in Tyrone were his infectious smile and his exuberant joy in the Lord. He seemed to be so consistently smiling and praising God for everything, to the extent that it initially seemed disingenuous. The more we were with them, the more he convinced us he was for real. His obvious love for his bride Alisha was genuine, and we were thrilled having them at our marriage conference. They had been married for 3 years when we first met them.

Before the conference was over, the Thorpe's spoke with us about the possibility of returning the following year to participate in a conference they would organize and manage, and we readily agreed. We believed their enthusiasm and energy was just the spark we needed for a very special meeting.

Throughout the summer and fall months we stayed in touch with the Thorpe's anticipating either a spring or early summer marriage retreat, which they would plan and coordinate. They set a date which was compatible with our schedule and made more complete preparations for the seminar, which included several other couples who would be in leadership roles. We agreed to be in prayer together for God's hand to be on the conference, and because we were separated by such a distance a conference call prayer meeting was scheduled for every 2 weeks for 2 months.

What an experience the conference call was for Cathy and me since we had not been part of such an event! There were at least 6 people on-line each time, and each was respectful of the one who was praying. It was thrilling for Cathy and me to be part of such a diversified group of believers whose sole purpose was to ask for God's blessing to be upon the marriage seminar.

The seminar was so well planned by Pastor Tyrone and Alisha it was by far the best marriage enrichment seminar we have ever been fortunate to attend. A highlight for us occurred on the evening prior to the start of the meeting when Cathy, Carolyn Lilley, and I joined Pastor Tyrone and Alisha for supper at the Golden Corral in Belleville, Illinois near the Thorpes' home. Our enthusiasm in that restaurant was fueled by the Thorpes', and especially Tyrone who seemed to witness to everyone present in that place. It was there that I was especially drawn to Tyrone's love for Jesus and his sincere desire to share the gospel with everyone.

Tyrone had been delivered years before from the deadly trap of alcohol, drugs, and the life-style they create. His life was a total wreck, including the breakup of his marriage and family and resulting in a prison sentence. By his testimony of hitting rock bottom and being homeless, his deliverance by the Lord Jesus was dramatic and complete. He had an intense and abiding heart interest for men and women who, like himself, were trapped by their sin and circumstances.

In addition to his deliverance from the deadly trap of sin, he was delivered from the initial effects of a head and neck cancer which had possibly resulted from his life-style choices. He received multiple irradiation treatments followed by chemotherapy, and for more than 5 years seemed to have been cured.

At some point following all of this, he met Alisha who was working as a nurse at the VA Hospital in St. Louis where he also worked. They began dating and decided it was God's will for them to be joined in marriage. Alisha had endured the harm from an abusive husband in her first marriage and through her faith and trust in the Lord Jesus had become a strong and faithful witness for Him. Tyrone and Alisha were made for each other and were married in 2011. Together they developed a ministry of hope and encouragement for any person who had been damaged by sin and their poor life-style choices. It was 3 years after their marriage that we first met them.

The final chapter in Tyrone's earthly life began in mid-2016 when he developed increasing symptoms of severe throat pain and difficulty in swallowing. He phoned me on several occasions, and we prayed together for each other. I was having increasing symptoms of heart disease and growing progressively weaker. Our times of prayer together by phone always encouraged me and drew me closer to the Lord Jesus which I heard in Tyrone's voice. He began the testing process which resulted in recommendation of a major surgical procedure to remove the recurrent head and neck cancer. Around the same time I was recommended to have open heart surgery.

As it turned out, our surgical procedures were on the exact same day: December 1, 2016. Tyrone was operated on at St. Louis University Hospital, and my procedure was done at Washington Regional Medical Center in Fayetteville, Arkansas. Had they not been on the same day, we would have been present at each other's hospital.

Tyrone's operation for complete cancer removal was not successful, and he grew increasingly worse from the cancer. Alisha faithfully cared for him day and night, using her nursing skills and doing many things which would normally be done by other health care providers. We stayed in touch as much as possible, and I gained enough strength for Cathy and I to travel to St. Louis to see him in the hospital in mid-April. He was so weak and couldn't talk because of his tracheotomy, but we saw that special twinkle in his eye and felt the mutual love in the handshake and ever-present smile. He was surrounded by family members, but we were able to stay for several hours, especially giving time for Cathy to spend time together with Alisha. I was fortunate to have about 30 minutes alone with Tyrone and Veronica, his lovely daughter from his first marriage. Veronica lives with her husband and children in Tampa, Florida, and she is a wonderful example of a Christian witness similar to her Father.

My brother Tyrone departed this life on April 26, 2017 at age60 years, and his spirit was immediately taken into the presence of His Savior the Lord Jesus Christ. I can only imagine the reverence and awe he experienced and can also visualize the enormous joy and gigantic smile which is now continually on his face. I miss him very much but am confident I will see that smile and sparkle in his eye once again. (I Thess.4:13-18)

Dr. John

MEET THE AUTHOR

Alisha Thorpe is a counselor, nurse, and ordained Evangelist who is passionate about sharing the Word of God and healing lives through the power of her testimony. She uses her incredible life experiences to draw people everywhere closer to God and to uplift, encourage, and edify. The daughter of Pentecostal parents, she was called by God at an early age to minister to His people. She is the co-founder of Faith Walk Ministry, a church without walls that caters to the homeless and the lost. She is also the founder of Faith, Family, and Friends, a Christian women's support organization, and she is the manager of Ministry Teen, a praise dance team. She has mentored countless women, and together with her late husband, Elder Howard Tyrone Thorpe, has counseled and supported a plethora of married couples. Evangelist Thorpe resides in Belleville, IL, where she continues to be active in her local ministry, *Love Church*, and in Nursing Home & Outreach ministries. *From Grief to Goodness* is her first publication.

Visit her website for more information www.alishathorpe.com